The Legend of the City of Ys

Charles Guyot

THE UNIVERSITY OF MASSACHUSETTS PRESS   Amherst, 1979

The Legend of the City of Ys

TRANSLATED AND ILLUSTRATED BY DEIRDRE CAVANAGH

INTRODUCTION BY MARIA TYMOCZKO

Published in French under the title La légende de la
ville d'Ys, d'après les anciens textes, *by Charles
Guyot, Eleventh edition, L'Édition d'Art, H. Piazza,
Paris, copyright © 1926 by H. Piazza. Translation,
Translator's Note, and Illustrations copyright © 1979
by Deirdre Cavanagh. Introduction copyright © 1979
by Maria Tymoczko*
Printed in the United States of America
Library of Congress Catalog Card Number 78-10235
ISBN 0-87023-264-9
Designed by Mary Mendell

Library of Congress Cataloging in Publication Data
Guyot, Charles.
The legend of the City of Ys.
*Translation of La légende de la ville d'Ys which is not
an original text but a retelling by the author.*
1. Is (Legendary city) I. Title.
GR941.I82G8913   1979   843'.9'12   78-10235
ISBN 0-87023-264-9

Contents

Introduction

Death and evil, supernatural beings and revenants, saints and devils are favorite themes of Breton folklore. All find a place in the legend of the city of Ys. The core of the story is simplicity itself: a city is submerged by an encroachment of the sea. In the elaboration of that simple nucleus, however, there is possibility for infinite variation and embellishment.

Stories of sunken cities are common in all Celtic-speaking countries and, indeed, are found throughout Europe.[1] In Wales one hears of Cantre'r Gwaelod, the Lowland Hundred submerged beneath Cardigan Bay; and of Llys Helig, the Court of Helig ap Glannawg identified in modern stories with rocks visible at the spring equinoctial tides beneath Conway Bay.[2] Such stories were popular in Wales as early as the Middle Ages. Not only does the Black Book of Carmarthen contain a ninth-century poem on Cantre'r Gwaelod,[3] but *Branwen*, one of the Four Branches of the *Mabinogi*, recounts how Bendigeidfran led his Welsh host on an invasion of Ireland:

> Bendigeidfran and the host of which we spoke sailed towards Ireland, and in those days the deep water was not wide. He went by wading. There were but two rivers, the Lli and the Archan were they called, but thereafter the deep water grew wider when the deep overflowed the kingdoms.[4]

Ireland also has stories of lands submerged beneath the sea, but more tantalizing are its related stories of rivers and lakes.[5] There is, for example, a story about the formation of the River Boyne (*Boand* in Irish) which occurred when Boand, wife of Nechtan, visited a well that only her husband and his cupbearers could tap safely. Three waves burst from the well, maiming the woman; then the water formed a river that pursued Boand to the sea where she was drowned.[6] This is actually a mythological story of submersion and destruction, for the characters are deities: Boand herself is a river goddess, and Nechtan (whose name is cognate with that of Neptune) is ostensibly a god, able to release and use, yet constrain and control, terrible waters.

The mythological dimension to eruptions of waters and sunken lands is echoed in Irish lake legends. In County Limerick there is Lough Gur, and its story has many similarities to the legend of the city of Ys:

> Lough Gur has been called the Enchanted Lake; some say that in ancient days there was a city where the lake is now, before an earthquake threw up the hills and filled the hollow with water so that the city was submerged. Even now, the peasants say, when the surface of the lake is smooth one may see from a boat, far down and down again, the drowned city, its walls and castle, houses and church, perfect and intact, waiting for the Day of Resurrection. And on Christmas eve, a dark night without moon and stars, if one looks down and down again, one may see lights in the windows, and listening with the ears of the mind, hear the muffled chiming of church bells.

The spirit of Lough Gur and its submerged lands is Ainë, the territorial goddess of that district of Ireland.[7]

Frequently in Irish tradition, realms under water are otherworldly.[8] Hence it is that the early Irish hero CuChulainn received his supernatural horses from lands beneath lakes, to which they returned upon his death.[9] Modern Irish folklore is filled with tales of dwellings beneath lakes and of lakes inhabited by supernatural creatures.[10] It is no wonder that Anglo-Irish writers have named the other world "Country-under-Wave."[11]

Breton tradition, likewise, has many stories of submerged lands; the city of Ys is not unique. Legends tell of forests swamped, cities drowned for their sins, and waters willfully loosed—often by a woman who perished for her deed.[12] There is even an echo of the story of Branwen in the report that at one time a person could walk to Jersey from the mainland, encountering only a narrow stream.[13]

It is against this varied, widespread, and longstanding tradition that we can assess the story of the city of Ys. The many versions of the destruction of Ker-Is—as it is called in Breton—converge in associating the legend with three names: Gradlon (also spelled Grallon and Gralon), Corentin, and Guenolé (also Guennolé, Gwénolé, Winwaloe). All are well-known figures in Breton tradition and are mentioned in early documents that serve as sources for Breton history: in the ninth-century *Life of Saint Guenolé* by Gourdisten (or Wrdisten), and in the eleventh-century cartulary of the monastery of Landévenec.[14]

In Gourdisten's *Life of Saint Guenolé*, Gradlon is called king of Cornouaille. He is reported to be stronger than any neighboring ruler and is celebrated for his victorious battles, including the defeat of "Northmen" in the area of the Loire. Gradlon is portrayed as a king who expanded the borders of his realm, one wealthy in lands, jewels, and booty.[15] He is given the byname *Meur* ('the Great') in the cartulary of Landévenec, and later rulers of Cornouaille are said to have borne his name.[16] Like other early Celtic kings, Gradlon appears to have been more a local tribal leader and warrior chieftain than a king in the modern sense of the word.

Corentin and Guenolé were saints, important in the development of the church of Cornouaille. Corentin traditionally is associated with the foundation of the episcopacy of Cornouaille, centered at Quimper.[17] Guenolé, about whose life much is known, was the founder and patron of Landévenec, one of the greatest Breton monasteries, situated on the Crozon peninsula.[18] Thus, the story of the city of Ys is anchored to the actions of historical characters who flourished at a definite point in time, the late fifth or early sixth century.[19]

The geography of the story is also usually precise, though it varies from version to version. The city of Ys is most often located in the Baie de Douarnenez, although the Baie des Trépassés is almost equally popular. At still other times the city is set in the Baie d'Audierne. Frequently tales will specify locations where individual episodes of the legend are said to have happened: places where the dead lovers of Dahut—the daughter of Gradlon—were discarded, where Gradlon's horse left hoofprints in the rock, and, above all, where Dahut herself was lost.

The geographical setting of the legend is appropriate: the city is set near the Pointe du Raz which faces westward to the open Atlantic. It is land's end, a wild and dangerous part of the Breton coast. The sea is rich and generous there; fish teeming on the shoals provide a good livelihood. But the reef that gives away its wealth also exacts its tribute. The passage between the land and the island of Sein, where the fishing is richest, is treacherous with strong currents. Until recently the inhabitants of the island lived by pirating wreckage, and the Baie des Trépassés ('Dead Men's Bay') was known for its toll of drowned men and the corpses that floated to shore there.[20]

These claims to historicity in the legend of Ker-Is—its historical characters, its definite time and place—are matched by details in Welsh legends. They do not, however, assure the historicity of the tale itself.[21] Neither Gourdisten's *Life of Saint Guenolé* nor the cartulary of Landévenec—the early documents that frame for us the existence and deeds of Gradlon, Corentin, and Guenolé—mentions the city of Ys or its destruction. Had a disaster of great magnitude occurred during Gradlon's time, we might expect it to be recorded in those documents.

Since *Ys* or *Is* is apparently a shortened form of *izel*, 'low,' *Ker-Is*, 'the city of Ys,' means simply 'the low town.'[22] Accordingly, it is possible to look for the historical kernel of the tale in the encroachment of the sea on villages or hamlets lying at sea level. Either storms or unusually high tides could at times wipe out such low-lying villages. With this view of things, a relatively restricted incident, or the conflation of several such episodes, is inflated and given tragic grandeur in part through association with a king.[23] This is, of course, a possible explanation for the tale of the city of Ys; but it is somewhat disappointing to think that this fine story is based on a rather minor historical event of only local importance.

The geology of Cap Sizun, the peninsula concerned, has yet to be established in relation to the legend. However, it is not likely that the sea has risen in that area some forty feet or more since Roman times—enough, for example, to cover the spire of a cathedral. An event of this magnitude would be recorded in documents, especially if it occurred suddenly, for it would have had more than a local impact.

There was, however, an actual time when the sea level was lower by forty feet or more than it is today. At the end of the last ice age, as the ice began to withdraw from Europe, the sea was in fact considerably lower—perhaps by as much as 400 feet—than it has been during the past 2,000 years.[24] A good deal more of the coastal shelf was exposed. It was even possible to walk from the continent all the way to Ireland via land bridges now covered by the English Channel and the Irish Sea. Flora and fauna spread over these bridges to the British Isles as the ice retreated. The first human inhabitants followed. Only gradually through the Neolithic period and the Bronze Age did the sea assume its present boundaries. As it did so, it swallowed up forest and bog, plains and fields and human habitations in low-lying areas.[25]

Thus, well within human experience the sea has made massive encroachments upon the land in northwestern Europe. The vast tracts of land engulfed during those early periods correspond to the sense of disaster and loss conveyed in the legend of the city of Ys and in other Celtic tales about sunken cities. We might then say that these legends of submersion are folk histories of actual events of the Stone Age and the Bronze Age.[26] Just as there are many aspects of Neolithic material culture that persist today in peasant life, so it is possible that folk memories of Stone Age times have lived on in the form of folk tales.[27] Those ancient tales may also have been assimilated to memories of more recent heroes like the king Gradlon.[28]

Tracing this legend back to the Stone Age might explain its popularity throughout all Celtic areas. These are areas whose borders were greatly affected by the rising seas in the first millenia of the last era. They are also areas that have preserved archaic customs and ancient beliefs—descended in some cases from Neolithic times—as well as a vigorous storytelling tradition which helped perpetuate ancient memories.[29]

The story of the city of Ys, then, belongs to tradition rather than to history. And it is in tradition, not in history, that one finds the fourth name most commonly associated with the legend—that of Dahut, Gradlon's daughter. Where she appears in the legend, Dahut is inevitably beautiful and evil. She leads the city of Ys in dissolute behavior, and she is frequently the cause, direct or indirect, of its destruction. In the end her own fate is bound up with that of the city.

Folk tradition about Dahut takes up where the story of the city of Ys leaves off. In folk tales Dahut is a siren with various manifestations. At times followed by a whale or floating above the submerged city, she lures men to their deaths and holds them in thrall in her watery realm.[30] She is beautiful, and her song is sweet.[31] She is often seen combing her blonde hair as she suns herself on the rocks. At times she is half fish, but in other reports she is a Mary-Morgan—a creature with a completely human body. The shape of the Mary-Morgans makes them even more treacherous than other sirens, and they are known for their evil. Near Tréguier, tradition says that all the sirens are descended from Dahut.[32] Dahut, then, is a character from folklore. Her name is found neither in historical documents like Gourdisten's *Life of Saint Guenolé* and the cartulary of Landévenec, nor is it found in the earliest versions of the legend of the city of Ys.

We have, seemingly, three historical figures—Gradlon, Corentin, Guenolé—and a folk character, the siren Dahut, bound in a single legend. But the gulf between Dahut and the others is not so great as it first appears, for the others also transcended the realm of strict historicity and came to figure in tales of all kinds. The process is already apparent in Gourdisten's *Life of Saint Guenolé*, where he refers to them as "three luminaries" (*candelis . . . ternis*) and "the three founders of Cornouaille" (*Cornubiae proceres . . . terni*). Gourdisten then goes on to comment at length on the special contributions each made to the realm.[33] The form of

Gourdisten's statement is itself significant; it is a triad, a genre used by native tellers in both Wales and Ireland to classify tales and lore.[34] The triad in Gourdisten's work indicates that by the ninth century, not only were tales told about these three, but also that by that time the three were associated with one another in popular tradition.

The elaboration of legends around the historical characters of the tale can be seen most clearly in the case of Gradlon.[35] Gourdisten's statement that Gradlon defeated the *Normanni*, the 'Northmen' (see p. ix above) is not based on historical fact but is a reflection of the saga-telling tastes of the ninth century: Gradlon, heroic king of another era, is pictured as triumphant over the imminent enemy of Gourdisten's contemporaries, the Northmen.[36] Gradlon's development as a legendary figure can also be traced in two forged charters included in the eleventh-century cartulary of Landévenec. One of these documents presents Gradlon receiving Charlemagne's messengers who ask for Gradlon's aid and promise him lands in perpetuity in exchange.[37] In a second charter, Gradlon receives gold and silver from Charlemagne's sons in lieu of the promised territory.[38] It may be that these charters reflect a lost epic associating Gradlon with the Carolingian monarchs at a period when French epic focused on Carolingian figures.[39] The charters suggest a narrative that showed the Breton king in a very favorable light, to the detriment, it would seem, of the Frankish emperor.[40] Thus, early in the development of Breton literature, Gradlon was an adaptable and protean figure.

Gradlon's development as an epic hero is paralleled by his roles in hagiography. He appears in the lives of the Saints Guenolé, Corentin, and Ronan, which in their earliest extant forms date from the ninth to the thirteenth centuries. In these lives Gradlon assumes stereotypical roles shared with other Celtic heroic figures who were introduced into hagiography.[41] He is alternately a noble king whose splendor is eclipsed by a still more noble saint, or a benefactor of the Church, or a rather unpleasant, tyrannical monarch.

We have evidence that by the end of the twelfth century yet another type of popular Celtic tale was told of Gradlon: the tale of a mortal's love for a fairy mistress and his departure with her to the other world.[42] Like other heroes, Gradlon (temporarily) lost his mistress when he revealed their union by a careless boast.[43] The story made its way from Breton tradition to Old French and survived as the *Lay of Graelant*. Once attributed to Marie de France (fl. 1165–85), the lay is now considered to be an independent work.[44]

Modern folk tradition about Gradlon indicates that he figured in other tale types as well. In popular tradition a tale has survived about

Gradlon's unusual birth and the manner in which he acquired his name.[45] These are traditional tales told about Celtic heroes.[46] Popular tradition also includes placelore telling how Gradlon's horse left its hoofprints on the Breton landscape.[47] Placelore about Celtic heroes is *de rigueur*; it is interesting that Arthur's dog, Cabal (whose name derives from *caballus*, 'horse'), also was said to have left his prints on rocks in Britain.[48] Stories of Gradlon's demise also follow familiar patterns: in the *Lay of Graelant*, Gradlon is taken to the other world beneath a river, and it is reported that some people say he is still alive; stories also report that at certain times of the year his phantom horse continues to be heard in the landscape; and still other folk tales suggest that Gradlon lies with Ys beneath the sea, yet to reawaken.[49] Such tales are reminiscent of the unresolved fate of Celtic heroes like Gerald the Earl in Ireland, who still feasts in his fairy mound and is doomed to ride through the countryside until the silver shoes on his horse wear out. And there are, of course, the more widespread stories of Arthur waiting in Avallon to return.

Gradlon emerges, then, as a traditional Celtic hero around whom many elements of Celtic storytelling coalesced in Brittany.[50] In this respect he is like King Arthur who in Welsh tradition gathered about him many types of tales and many characters originally independent of Arthurian lore.[51] Gradlon, like Arthur in Britain, came to represent the sovereignty of his people; at times the first king recorded in early chronicles, Gradlon is the only one remembered in popular tales.[52] His prowess was celebrated in epic tales; he was a foil in hagiography; he figured in triads and placelore; he was the hero of a fairy-mistress story; his exploits were signalled by special birth and name-giving; his death was unresolved. The more a hero becomes a focus of tradition, the more likely he is to attract popular tales that once circulated independently of him. It is no wonder that Breton tales about sirens and sunken cities came to be associated with Gradlon.[53]

Let us examine briefly what can be surmised about the development of the story of the city of Ys. The earliest reference to the tale that can be dated with certainty is found in Bertrand d'Argentré's *L'histoire de Bretaigne* (*The History of Britanny*, 2nd ed., 1588):[54]

> Some have written that during the life of this king the city of Ys, near Kemper, was engulfed and submerged by the sea. Still today the local people point out the ruins and the remains of the walls, so well mortared that the sea has not been able to carry them away, and they say that the king Gradlon was in it at the time when it was ruined. Those are accidents which have often happened elsewhere by similar

encroachments of the sea, and God saved Lot from a similar fate. But of those things there is no witness but an old rumor noised from person to person.[55]

This early version is significant for its simplicity: it may represent the form of the story current in sixteenth-century oral tradition. Argentré makes it clear that he was familiar with the oral tradition about the city, and that such tales were well established and widespread by his time. Note that in this version, the city is destroyed by a simple accident of nature in which Gradlon apparently dies. The themes of corruption and punishment are absent, and there is no reference to Dahut or Guenolé. Neither saints nor sinners play a role.

A first phase of elaboration of the oral core is reflected in a group of early Breton mystery plays on the life of Saint Guenolé.[56] All derive ultimately from a 1580 text, but the original itself has been lost. It is represented by a copy made in the eighteenth century, as well as later adaptations from the seventeenth and eighteenth centuries which modified the early text in various ways. In all versions of the mystery play the submersion of the city of Ys is a central event that occupies a substantial portion of the text.[57] Thus, this version of the story is detailed and well articulated. The plays present Ys explicitly as a "modern" Sodom and Gomorrah. It is a city that has rejected God. Its inhabitants enjoy every evil and they are ultimately punished by flood, just like Noah's contemporaries. The flood strikes only after Guenolé—preaching repentance like Jonah and Jeremiah—warns of the disaster and offers them a chance to reform their ways; he is summarily rejected. Gradlon—like the biblical Lot—is the one person who hearkens to the message, and who is saved from destruction by a messenger of the Lord, here Guenolé.[58]

In the mystery plays, then, the tale became an episode of a saint's life, where the themes of evil, the call to repentance, and the motif of divine retribution seem rather congenial, especially with their explicit biblical parallels. Guenolé is the hero of this version of the story of Ker-Is, and his prestige is deliberately increased by his role in saving Gradlon and his moral direction of Gradlon. The plays have subsumed the legend of the city of Ys to Gradlon's customary roles in hagiography, including his other relations to Guenolé (see p. xii, above): splendid but errant king who is morally subordinated to the saints, and becomes in the end a benevolent prop and patron of the church. The Christian dimensions of the legend of Ker-Is, represented in these texts for the first time, molded the story in significant ways. Many became standard features in later presentations of the tale.

In 1636 Albert le Grand (also known as Albert de Morlaix) published

Les vies des saints de la Bretagne armorique (*The Lives of the Saints of Brittany*). In the life of Saint Guenolé, Le Grand included an account of the destruction of the city of Ys. As it appeared in the first edition of his work, the story of Ker-Is was similar to the Christianized accounts in the extant mystery plays.[59] Together they probably represent a related tradition, and they show that throughout the first half of the seventeenth century, there was a widespread version of the legend which had developed religious overtones and featured Saint Guenolé as a major character.[60]

Another step in the development of the legend can be seen in the third edition of Le Grand's work, published in 1680.[61] For the first time Dahut was given a role in the city's destruction; thus we can pinpoint the mid-seventeenth century as the period when she was attached to the legend.[62] The legend as it appeared in the third edition was the basis of later reprints of Le Grand's treatment of the tale, and has remained the most famous early version of the story of the city of Ys. It is translated here *in extenso*:

> [Guennolé] went often to see the king Grallon in the proud City of Is and preached very openly against the abominations that were being committed in that great city which was completely absorbed in luxury, debauchery, and vanity and which remained obstinate in their sins. God revealed to Saint Guennolé the just punishment he wished to bring.
>
> Saint Guennolé had gone to see the king, as was his habit. While they were speaking together, God revealed to him that the hour of chastisement had come which would make a lesson of the inhabitants of that city. The saint, as if returning from rapture and ecstasy, said to the king, "Ah, Sire, Sire! Let us leave this place as fast as possible, for the wrath of God is going to overwhelm it presently. Your majesty knows the dissolutions of this populace. It has been vain to preach to them; the measure is filled. They must be punished. Let us haste to leave or otherwise we will be gathered and caught in this same misfortune."
>
> The king without delay had his baggage packed. Having put out all he held most dear, he mounted a horse and with his officers and servants, at a gallop he fled out of the city. Hardly had he passed the gates when a violent storm arose with winds so wild that the sea, leaping from its normal boundaries and casting itself furiously on that miserable city, covered it in no time, drowning many thousands of people.
>
> The principal cause was attributed to the princess Dahut, immodest daughter of the good king, who perished in that gulf and who

attempted to cause the death of the king in a spot that still has the name Toul-Dahut or Toul-Alc'huez, that is, 'Dahut's Hole' or 'The Hole of the Keys,' for the story asserts that she had taken from her father the key that he wore hanging about his neck as symbol of the sovereignty.

The king, having fled on time, went to stay at Land-Tevenec with Saint Guennolé whom he thanked for this deliverance. Thereafter he withdrew to Kemper.[63]

This first reference to Dahut is a surprisingly detailed account, implying as it does her lechery (*fille impudique*, 'immodest daughter'), and narrating both her usurpation of a key that symbolized sovereignty, and her death. One of the most interesting elements is the reference to Toul-Dahut as the place where she attempted to cause the death of her father. It shows that by the second half of the seventeenth century, there was already placelore about Dahut and, moreover, that the placelore associated her with the destruction or attempted destruction of men.[64] In later centuries the place was remembered simply as the site of her drowning. Though the allusion to Dahut is brief, it shows that the legend had developed considerably in the half century that separates this text from the first edition of Albert le Grand's *Vies des saints de la Bretagne armorique*. Note, too, that the references to Dahut—particularly her attempted destruction of her father—show that her characterization retained primitive elements suggestive of a siren's nature.

A third early version of the story is worth quoting in its entirety. This tale was included by Jacques Cambry in *Voyage dans le Finistère ou l'état de ce département en 1794 et 1795* (*A Trip through Finistere, or the State of this Department in 1794 and 1795*):

> The proud city of Is—thus it is that the legends, hymns, and bards of Brittany speak of it—was under the rule of the king Gralon; all types of luxury and debauchery reigned in that opulent city. In vain there the friends of God, the most holy persons preached morals and reform. Saint Guenolé himself wasted his breath there. The princess Dahut, daughter of the king, forgetting the modesty and moderation natural to her sex, gave example there of all sorts of depravity.
>
> The hour of vengeance arrived: the calm that precedes the most awful storms, song, music, lovemaking, wine, all types of spectacle and debauchery intoxicated and lulled the hardened inhabitants of the great city. King Gralon, he alone, was not inattentive to the voice of Heaven. He attended church services and kept company with the servants of God.

One day Saint Guenolé, seized like the prophets or the Sibyls of Cumae, in a solemn voice pronounced these words before the king Gralon.

"Prince, disorder has reached a pinnacle, the hand of the Eternal One is raised, the sea is swelling, the city of Is is going to disappear. Let us depart."

Gralon, obedient to the voice of the holy man, is on horse, fleeing at full speed. His daughter Dahut is riding behind him on the horse. The hand of the Eternal One falls; the highest towers of the city are engulfed, howling waves press the steed of the saintly king who is unable to free himself. A terrible voice is heard, "Prince, if you wish to save yourself, shake off the devil who sits behind you."

Whether the prince obeyed and whether he drowned his daughter, whether the princess sacrificed herself for her father by throwing herself off, whether Lucifer seized Dahut in order to spare the prince the pain of drowning her, I do not know. The historians of the time have not related the deed well, and commentators have neglected to clear it up.

Beautiful Dahut lost her life—drowned near the place called Poul-Dahut. The storm ceased, the air became calm, Heaven serene. But since that time the vast basin along which a part of the city of Ys stretched has been covered with water. It is the Baie de Douarnenez.

I have been shown on the bank near Ris an irrefutable monument of that terrible event. It is a rock called Garrec on which is printed the foot of Gralon's horse. . . .[65]

Several aspects of this version merit comment. First, Cambry's account follows the main lines of the story laid down in the seventeenth century: the city is a nest of evil, the saints attempt its reform, Dahut leads in depravity, only Gradlon remains uncorrupt, Guenolé prophesies the destruction and warns the king to flee, the destruction takes the form of a sudden storm. Cambry also gives evidence that the story—presumably as he tells it—was popular in oral tradition in his day. Thus, he refers to Breton "legends [and] hymns." He also lists a series of variants concerning the demise of Dahut, variants that all reappear in nineteenth-century versions of the tale.

Two elements of the story appear to have been expanded in the century between Albert le Grand's third edition and Cambry's version. According to Cambry, the disaster is said to have struck at a time of merriment; this motif coincides with Welsh tales about sunken cities where the disaster strikes during a feast.[66] More important, however, is the final sequence: Dahut, riding behind her father, is drowned after a voice commands her father to shake her off.[67] Together with the placelore about Poul-Dahut and the calming of the sea after Dahut's death, this sequence came to be the accepted mode of ending the story.

From these early versions we see that the legend was in the process of growth throughout the sixteenth, seventeenth, and eighteenth centuries. It began as a rather simple oral tale, and gradually expanded in detail. It became shaped by Christian and moral concerns, incorporating along the way Dahut, a legendary Mary-Morgan, peril to men's bodies and souls.[68]

These early versions of the legend of the city of Ys tend to focus on Saint Guenolé and on moralistic lessons. Goodness and justice triumph, wickedness is punished, and no sympathy is accorded those who stray from the path of righteousness. Thus, in the seventeenth and eighteenth centuries the tale of Ker-Is was an exemplum, a cautionary tale. It was also a tale whose appeal was restricted to Breton audiences.

It remained for the nineteenth century to do quite different things with the legend of the city of Ys. We can trace the modern development of the legend to Emile Souvestre who published two versions of the tale: a brief version in *En Bretagne (In Brittany)*, and a fuller version in his 1844 volume of Breton folktales, *Le foyer breton (The Breton Hearth)*.[69] Souvestre's versions unite in a single narrative the motifs and the emphases that characterize subsequent retellings of the story. Significant motifs appear if not for the first time in his work, then for the first time in concatenation.[70] In his versions the city of Ys is protected from the sea by a dike and locks which are opened by a fateful key.[71] Destruction of the city is not a punitive act of God manifest in storm and sudden wave. It is deliberate and willful destruction that comes from within: the locks are opened and the sea is invited into the city either by Dahut herself (*En Bretagne*) or by her satanic lover (*Le foyer breton*).

In Souvestre's hands the emphasis of the story and the thematic development change dramatically. We have already seen that in the seventeenth and eighteenth centuries the story was an exemplum presenting clear moral lessons. The heroes were the virtuous; Dahut was given a restricted role when she was mentioned at all. But in Souvestre's versions, Dahut plays a larger role; the focus is on her evil deeds rather than on the exemplary ones of Gradlon or the saints. This focus is reflected in the elaboration of material about Dahut. In Souvestre's shorter version she is immediately identified as evil:

[Dahut] was the Honoraria of Armorica. Like the daughter of Valentinian "she made a crown for herself of her vices, and had taken as her pages the seven deadly sins." In her monstrous devices [she fore-shadowed] Marguerite de Bourgogne of the tower of Nesle. . . .[72]

We read the details of her sins: her nightly lovers, the treacherous mask which strangles them after she has taken her pleasure, her black servant who disposes of the corpses by dumping them in a pit. Dahut is not only presented here as seductive and sexually attractive, but also as one who flouts authority. In *En Bretagne* she wrongly appropriates the key to the dike—the sign of authority—from her father and ruler.[73] Dahut is a femme fatale bent on destruction including, perversely, her own.

There is a fascination with evil and destruction in Souvestre's narratives that is heightened by his emphasis on and celebration of the beauty and wealth of the city itself:

> popular tradition teaches us that [Ys] was a great city enriched by commerce, embellished by the arts, and so important that it was thought an honor to call old Lutèce *Par-is*, that is, the equal of the Breton city. . . . The palace of the king was one of the marvels of the earth; marble, cedar, and gold there replaced oak, granite, and iron. . . .[74]

Souvestre's longer version differs from the shorter in several significant ways. In one of his most striking additions, Souvestre informs the reader:

> Since [Dahut] was a great magician, she had embellished the city with works one could not expect from the hand of man. All the korigans of Cornouaille and Vanne had come at her order to construct the dikes and forge the doors which were of iron; they had covered the palace with a metal like gold (for the korigans are skillful counterfeiters) and had surrounded the gardens with railings that shone like polished steel. It was they who tended Dahut's stables, paved with black, red or white marble to match the color of the horses, and they who maintained the port where the sea-dragons were fed. For Dahut with her art had tamed the monsters of the sea and given one to each inhabitant of Keris who used them like steeds to seek rare merchandise across the waves or to attack enemy vessels. . . .[75]

Traditions about the korigans were widespread in Brittany throughout the nineteenth century and continue to circulate in the present. Stories about them are similar to stories about *an sluagh sidhe*, the Irish fairies. Often the korigans are dangerous or harmful to human beings—stealing children or brides, damaging animals, bringing bad luck or death—but they can be beneficent as well. It is interesting to note that in Breton folklore, fairies and sirens often have good relations with one another.[76] It may be that those good relations are echoed in Souvestre's report that the korigans were instrumental in constructing the city of Ys, given Dahut's connection with legends about sirens.

Souvestre wrote his versions of the Ys legend at the height of French romanticism, and they suited the times. They were literary retellings of the tale, but Souvestre invoked as his source in *En Bretagne* "la tradition populaire" ('popular tradition'). Similarly, his longer version of the story is entitled, "Récit du vieux pecheur" ("The Old Fisherman's Tale"): "KerIs" is a subtitle.[77] Souvestre's emphasis on his popular sources is part of his romantic appeal.

The early nineteenth century was a time of great interest in "the folk" as well as in all types of "primitive" cultures. These interests central to romanticism found many outlets, including the collection of popular oral tales. At the time when native cultures of the New World were being investigated, and the medieval heritage of the Old World was being reclaimed, interest naturally turned to neglected fields at home. In particular, the Celts were "discovered"; their discovery was spurred by the 1761–65 publication of MacPherson's *Works of Ossian* and a half-century of literary controversy surrounding MacPherson. Interest in all aspects of Irish, Welsh, and Scottish literature, history, and popular tradition was alive in the nineteenth century. There was even a revived interest in local flood legends.[78]

In this cultural milieu, Souvestre's work could have been only a success. Amidst a general fascination with the Celts, he introduced the neglected Celtic culture of Brittany. The "basse-Bretons," earlier the butt of ridicule for French culture, were presented instead as the peasant guardians of exotic ancient memories and heroic tales. Moreover, Souvestre wrote in French for French audiences; and he offered them French Celts in lieu of British Celts. Add to this the invocation of local Celtic folk, the themes of good and evil, luxury and corruption, the hint of lost grandeur, and the overall tone of tragedy, and his legends of the city of Ys were destined to have widespread appeal.

From Souvestre's time to the present, the story of the city of Ys has been told and retold. A steady stream of versions appeared throughout the nineteenth century. Although we cannot consider them all in any detail in this brief survey, two nineteenth-century versions are of particular interest: those of Hersart de la Villemarqué and V. Le Breton de la Haize.

One of the most interesting and, in ways, amusing chapters in the emergence of Breton literature in the nineteenth century centers around the publication of La Villemarqué's *Barzaz-Breiz, chants populaires de la Bretagne* (*Popular Songs of Brittany*). The book appeared in three rather different editions (1839, 1845, 1867), the last two of which contain a poem relating to Ker-Is. "La submersion de la ville d'Is" ("The Submersion of the City of Is"), as the poem is called, was one of thirty-three historical ballads introduced into the second edition of *Barzaz-Breiz*; most of the new material has a political tone celebrating the Celtic culture of Brittany in opposition to French culture.[79]

La Villemarqué's version of the legend is only fifty-seven lines long, most of which is dialogue. Hence, the content is quite abbreviated. It is nonetheless a striking and dramatic poem that includes a catchy warning to the inhabitants of the city: "Who eats the flesh of fish will be eaten by fish. . . ."[80] The formulaic wording was attractive despite a nonspecific meaning that could apply to an entire fishing population. Similarly, there is a pathetic description of Dahut's theft of the keys from her father. The sleeping king is described in lines reminiscent of descriptions of Charlemagne in *The Song of Roland*.[81] The poem purports to be a song, and La Villemarqué provided a melody for his readers.

La Villemarqué's work gives every sign of being based upon authentic remnants of Breton tradition. Breton texts are presented with French translations, and copious scholarly notes accompany the collection. The poems were hailed throughout France; *Barzaz-Breiz* was a sensation in the artistic and intellectual world. George Sands declared that one of the poems, "Le tribut de Noménoë" ("The Tribute of Nominoë"), was superior to *The Iliad* and represented the masterpiece of the human spirit. The poetry of Brittany, she continued, achieved the pinnacle of genius even when compared with any nation on earth.[82]

After a period of initial acceptance, despite the Breton texts and the scholarly apparatus, *Barzaz-Breiz* sparked a repeat of the controversy that had raged around MacPherson: were La Villemarqué's texts authentic or were they his own productions? It is generally agreed now that like MacPherson's books, La Villemarqué's work was primarily his own creation.[83] For Breton letters, however, that judgment is perhaps less significant than the fact that La Villemarqué's work was widely known, that he—like Souvestre—stimulated widespread interest in Breton literature, and that the controversy over the authenticity of his poems resulted in efforts to collect and preserve genuine Breton material. It is clear that the popularity of *Barzaz-Breiz*—including as it did after 1845 a version of the legend of the city of Ys—did much to spread this particular tale to a broad public. Throughout the nineteenth century, La Villemarqué's text on Ker-Is was frequently reproduced or quoted, and it was his text of the tale that was translated at an early date for an English-speaking audience.[84]

The last nineteenth-century version of the legend to concern us is much less well known than the creations of either Souvestre or La Villemarqué. In 1854 Le Vicomte Le Breton de la Haize published *Moeurs et coutumes de l'ancienne Armorique ou légendes bretonnes en vers* (*Manners and Customs of Ancient Armorica, or Breton Legends in Verse*).[85] Included in the collection, in rather irregular, rimed French verse, is a very curious version of the legend of the city of Ys. Gradlon is presented as an old and feeble man whose power has passed to his beautiful and proud daughter. She recants her Christianity and returns to druidical rites. As a priestess herself she sacrifices human victims to Teutates. She oppresses Christianity with pillage and fire, taking altar vessels for her banquets.

Le Breton de la Haize speaks through the bards and druids of the poem: Dahut is praised for returning to the old ways which will ensure a return to Gaul of "happiness, power, and liberty." Dahut proclaims, "once again our warlike ranks will subject the world to our laws."[86] Guenolé thwarts these grand designs by calling for repentance and then cursing Dahut. The flaccid Gradlon is rescued by the saint just before a tidal wave swamps both the city and Dahut.

This version of the story is of interest principally because of its opposition between Christianity and pagan religion, in particular druidism. The early mystery plays had suggested a similar opposition, but the emphasis in the plays is chiefly on recanting Christianity. Where pagan gods are mentioned in the plays, they are the idols from epic tradition—Roman gods and Christian devils.[87] Le Breton de la Haize, on the other hand, substitutes druid cults and obliquely glorifies a return to Celtic religion. Thus, in his hands, Dahut's development took another step—the siren become magician (cf. p. xix, above) is a ruthless, warlike, pagan priestess.

This version is a prototype of one development of the tale of Ker-Is— a strand represented also by a famous song written by Olivier Souêtre (also Souvestre). Souêtre's song appeared anonymously in 1850 as sheet music; and it became enormously popular, remaining so until World War I. It is an example of a literary work that reentered popular tradition to be actually adopted by "the folk." Souêtre's song, like the poem of Le Breton de la Haize, had references to druidism, including the worship of Teutates.[88]

Versions of the destruction of the city of Ys proliferated after 1850. The tale found its way into guidebooks and general works on Brittany. Often the authors of these derivative works produced still new versions by conflating or combining older ones. Through such manuals, however, the tale achieved currency outside its Breton setting and entered the realm of European letters as a whole.

The story of Ys was only one of many Breton tales popular in the nineteenth century. It was, however, a tale that artists of all disciplines found particularly stimulating. Writers were seized by its spell—Victor Hugo himself considered writing about the city of Ys, though he did not in fact undertake the project.[89] Artists painted the scene—and still today in the museum at Quimper a painting by Luminais evokes the disaster.[90] The story had some of its more illustrious extensions in music. In 1888 Lalo produced an opera on the theme, called *Le roy d'Ys* (*The King of Ys*). It was followed in 1910 by Debussy's *La cathédrale engloutie* (*The Sunken Cathedral*).

If I have lingered over the nineteenth-century development of the legend, it is because that development underlies our present understanding of the tale. Nineteenth-century treatments share certain common traits and contrast markedly with earlier versions. We have seen that the seventeenth and eighteenth centuries presented the story as an exemplum. In the versions of those centuries, the focus was on saints or exemplary figures like Gradlon. Dahut was merely an ancillary character.

Throughout the nineteenth century, on the other hand, Dahut came to play a larger and larger role. In many nineteenth-century versions, she is clearly the central character. Her excesses, whether sexual or religious, are a good deal more interesting than the rather pale moral elements in romantic treatments of the story. Surely this change in the legend is related to the nineteenth-century fascination with evil. In French letters alone the theme echoes from Balzac's *La peau de chagrin* (*The Wild Ass's Skin*) to Dumas's *La tour de Nesle* (*The Tower of Nesle*), from the enthusiastic reception of Poe with his focus on the perverse, to Baudelaire's *Les fleurs du mal* (*The Flowers of Evil*).

Nineteenth-century versions of the story were touched by romanticism in different ways. Exotic elements were heightened in a variety of forms—from the involvement of fairies to the chanting of druids. Significantly, the entire tone of the story changed. The legend ceased to be a divine comedy and a moral victory; it became a human tragedy. Each nineteenth-century version resounds with the loss of a strange and terrible beauty.

Nineteenth-century versions are also characterized by being definitively literary. They sprang from the individual imagination, and they entered the realm of literary tradition. It is worth noting that the literary tradition they entered was a French, not a Breton, tradition: what was originally an oral Breton tale became a literary French story in the course of the last century.

In 1926 Charles Guyot published *La légende de la ville d'Is (The Legend of the City of Is)*. The English translation of Guyot's version appears in the following pages for the first time. Guyot's retelling of the destruction of the city of Ys is one of the longest, most graceful, and most literary of all the versions. The main lines of his story follow the romantic presentation of the legend. Dahut is clearly the central figure; her relation to the sea binds the work into a whole. This relationship, one of the finest elements of his creation, guided Guyot in his choice of variants and his interpretation of episodes.[91] He is heavily dependent on Souvestre's longer version of the story for his plot, but he echoes both La Villemarqué and the versions that feature an opposition between Christianity and Celtic religion.[92] However, Guyot reached beyond these modern elaborations to include earlier material as well. Hence it is that the saints play so large a role in his story. He followed the saints' lives by Le Grand carefully and fully.[93] At the same time many other elements in Guyot's tale have no source but his own imagination and the power of his creation.[94] Thus, the book should be read as a story, not as a document—a story that strives for fullness and beauty, as Guyot says in his introduction.

Guyot also states in his introduction that oral tradition kept the tale alive. It is true that there are many popular tales about Ker-Is. The oral tales, however, generally presuppose the destruction of the city rather than narrate its downfall. Moreover, even when oral tales do narrate the inundation, they rarely preserve ancient tradition. We have seen that the development of the tale can be traced in written texts. These literary inventions, in turn, passed into oral tradition to remake and alter beyond recognition the early core of the tale.[95] However, throughout the nineteenth century other types of folk tales were collected about the city of Ys—tales that assert the city did not die, but lies beneath the waves to rise again one day. Sightings of the city and encounters with its inhabitants are frequently narrated, for the city of Ys can only rise, it is said, through mortal agency.[96]

Popular tradition neither savors the wickedness of the city as nineteenth-century literary versions do, nor condemns the wickedness as seventeenth- and eighteenth-century versions are wont. Rather, popular tradition skirts the question of evil, remembering Ker-Is chiefly for its beauty and its might:

My mother saw the city of Is rise over the water. It was all castles and turrets. In the façades there were thousands of windows. The roofs were shining and bright as if they were of crystal. She could hear distinctly the bells ringing in the churches and the murmur of the crowd in the streets.[97]

And again: "In Is there were a hundred cathedrals, and in each one there was a bishop officiating."[98] This city of one hundred churches is a kind of other world, a splendid Country-under-Wave. Like the ancient Celtic other world, its existence is parallel to our own but accessible to mortals only under strange and perilous circumstances.

The otherworldly quality of the drowned city may have mythological roots. Occasionally a folk tale will have an archaic touch—like the crystal in the description above.[99] In another story the rush of waters that overwhelmed the city is said to have come from a well.[100] That report echoes the Welsh tale of Cantre'r Gwaelod and the Irish tale of the Boyne recorded a millenium earlier.

But what may have once been a mythological other world has come also to represent a political other world. The city of Ys is a figure of the lost freedom and power of an independent Brittany ruled by its own leaders. Some have even said that should Ker-Is be saved, should it awaken and rise, Paris would be eclipsed and have to cede its primacy.[101] Ker-Is offers an eternal vision. Like all otherworldly things, it is ancient memory and future hope:

> Ker-Ys is the Brittany of today submerged beneath the waters of an alien civilization; but the time is coming, though the manner is as yet unknown, when Ker-Ys shall be restored to its supremacy, when its carillons shall again ring and its streets and churches be thronged with happy crowds. . . . Brittany shall again be a land ruled by its own rulers, contented in its independence . . . Ker-Ys, beneath the waves. . . , holds out the promise of a Brittany triumphant.[102]

The story of the city of Ys, so simple in its core, has adapted to many times and many moods. As Celtic mythological other world or Christian exemplum, as the exploration of evil or political allegory, it proves an enduring and arresting tale.

NOTES

1. See the references in Stith Thompson, *Motif-Index of Folk-Literature*, 2nd. ed. (Bloomington, 1955), under F 944 "City sinks in the sea" and F 944.1 "City sinks in sea or lake as punishment." Related motifs include F 941.2.2 "Church and congregation sink to bottom of sea"; A 920.1.8 "Lake bursts forth to drown impious people"; F 725 "Submarine world"; F 725.2 "Submarine cities"; F 725.3 "Submarine castle (palace)"; F 760 "Extraordi-

nary cities"; F 133 "Submarine otherworld"; D 789.8 "Disenchantment of sunken castle/town"; D 791.3 "Disenchantment fails because conditions are not fulfilled"; and Q 220 "Impiety punished."

2. A collection of Welsh legends of submersion by the sea and lakes is found in John Rhŷs, *Celtic Folklore, Welsh and Manx*, 2 vols. (Oxford, 1901), "Folklore of the Wells," 1:354–400, and "Triumphs of the Water-World," 2:401–55. F. J. North has published an excellent survey of the Welsh legends, in *Sunken Cities, Some Legends of the Coast and Lakes of Wales* (Cardiff, 1957). North's study gives a critical review of the growth of the legends, and he discusses their relationship to geological data.

3. A translation and discussion of the ninth-century poem appears in Rachel Bromwich's excellent article (to which I am indebted), "Cantre'r Gwaelod and Ker-Is" in *The Early Cultures of North-West Europe* (*H. M. Chadwick Memorial Studies*), ed. Cyril Fox and Bruce Dickins (Cambridge, 1950), pp. 217–41.

4. Gwyn Jones and Thomas Jones, trans., *The Mabinogion* (1949; reprint ed., New York, 1963), p. 33. *Branwen* is an eleventh-century text.

5. For Irish legends involving encroachment of the sea see Seán Ó Súilleabháin, *A Handbook of Irish Folklore* (1942; reprint ed., Detroit, 1970), pp. 501, 506.

6. Whitley Stokes, ed. and trans., "The Prose Tales in the Rennes Dindsenchas," *Revue Celtique* 15 (1894): 315–16.

7. Mary Carbery, *The Farm by Lough Gur* (1937; reprint ed., Cork, 1973), pp. 13–14; see Proinsias MacCana, *Celtic Mythology* (New York, 1970), pp. 86, 131, for a brief discussion of Ainë.

8. See the references listed in T. P. Cross, *Motif-Index of Early Irish Literature* (Bloomington, 1952), under F 133 "Submarine Otherworld." Howard Rollin Patch calls this reflex of the Celtic otherworld "Land-beneath-the-Waves," and summarizes references to it in *The Otherworld According to Descriptions in Medieval Literature* (Cambridge, Mass., 1950), passim. See also T. F. O'Rahilly, *Early Irish History and Mythology* (Dublin, 1946), pp. 14, 262, 291 n.4.

9. George Henderson, ed. and trans., *Fled Bricrend, The Feast of Bricriu* (London, 1899), pp. 38–39; and Maria Tymoczko, trans., *Two Death Tales from the Ulster Cycle: The Death of CuRoi and the Death of CuChulainn* (Dublin, 1979), forthcoming.

10. Ó Súilleabháin, *Handbook*, pp. 500–507; and Máire MacNeill, *The Festival of Lughnasa* (Oxford, 1962), pp. 147, 155, 164 ff., 179 ff., 195 ff., 208, 223, 243–86, 314 ff.

11. W. B. Yeats, *The Variorum Edition of the Plays of W. B. Yeats*, ed. Russell K. Alspach, assisted by Catharine C. Alspach (New York, 1966), pp. 91, 485, 508, 511, 549, 559. The term is translated from the Irish *tír fo thuinn*.

12. Paul Sébillot, *Légendes locales de la Haute-Bretagne* (Nantes, 1899), 1:18–30.

13. Ibid., p. 23.

14. Both documents are found in Arthur de la Borderie, ed., *Cartulaire de l'abbaye de Landevenec* (Rennes, 1888). The historical value of these documents has been hotly debated. La Borderie has argued for their value, and he based his chronology of early Breton history on them. For his arguments and his reconstruction of Breton history, see "Le cartulaire de Landevenec," *Annales de Bretagne* 4 (1888–89): 295–364, and his *Histoire de Bretagne* (Rennes, 1896), 1:311–34.

Robert Latouche, *Mélanges d'histoire de Cornouaille (v^e–xie siècle)* (Paris, 1911), has argued the contrary position, maintaining that the documents are of no historical value. Gilbert H. Doble, "Saint Winwaloe," *The Saints of Cornwall*, (Cornish Saints Series no. 4, 2nd ed., 1940; rept. ed., Oxford, 1962), pp. 64–66, 75–76, together with the important references he has cited there, provides the most recent assessment of the question.

15. La Borderie, *Cartulaire*, pp. 78–79 (bk. 2, chaps. 15–16).

16. Ibid., p. 172 (charter no. 54). He is also called *magnus* in Gourdisten's *Life of Saint Guenolé*, ibid, p. 75 (bk. 2, chap. 12). French translations of the relevant passages of the cartulary and the *Life of Saint Guenolé* can be found in La Borderie, *Histoire*, pp. 312–24. Cf. Arthur de la Borderie, "Gradlon-Mur," *Biographie bretonne*, ed. Prosper-Jean Levot (Vannes, 1852), 1:830–35.

17. A summary and assessment of the life of Saint Corentin is given by Gilbert H. Doble, "Saint Corentin," *The Saints of Cornwall* (Cornish Saints Series no. 5, 1925; rept. ed., Oxford, 1962), pp. 44–53. The life of Saint Corentin is probably from the thirteenth century, and it is not of great historical value.

18. Doble, "Saint Winwaloe," pp. 59–108.

19. Bromwich, "Cantre'r Gwaelod," pp. 239–40.

20. The whole area, probably because of its striking geography, is associated with legends, sayings, and folk prayers, many of which are ancient. Cf. Augustus Hare, *North-Western France (Normandy and Brittany)* (London, 1895), pp. 388–92.

21. Cf. the discussion of the historicity of the Welsh legends in North, *Sunken Cities*, pp. 54–70, 170–75; and Bromwich, "Cantre'r Gwaelod," pp. 221–31.

22. Bromwich, "Cantre'r Gwaelod," p. 235 n.2, notes that the name is parallel to *Cantre'r Gwaelod* which means 'the bottom cantref' or 'the lowland cantref.'

23. This view was put forth as early as 1752 by Le Pelletier, quoted in Louis Ogès, "La légende de la ville d'Is," *Nouvelle revue de Bretagne*, no. 2 (1949): 83. More recently it was proposed by W. Branch Johnson, *Folktales of Brittany* (London, 1927), pp. 48–49.

24. North, *Sunken Cities*, p. 198.

25. Ibid., chaps. 5, 10. North gives a detailed discussion of the change in sea level since the last ice age. He relates the geological phenomena of the Welsh coast to the Welsh legends of inundation.

26. J. E. Lloyd, *A History of Wales from the Earliest Times to the Edwardian Conquest*, 3rd ed. (London, 1939), p. xxxii, has proposed a similar argument with reference to Welsh legends of submersion. I am indebted for this reference to Bromwich, "Cantre'r Gwaelod," p. 227 n.4.

North, *Sunken Cities*, chap. 10, especially pp. 205–10, cf. pp. 241–45, also traces the Welsh legends to Neolithic experience, but he prefers to see the legends as reflecting incidents of sudden local submersion during the Neolithic period and the Bronze Age.

Bromwich, "Cantre'r Gwaelod," pp. 227, 231, 241, on the other hand, thinks the legends originated in a desire to explain striking local topographical details. In this she concurs with Alexander Haggerty Krappe, *The Science of Folklore* (New York, 1930), pp. 70–74. According to this view, the similarities in the legends are a result of polygenesis (attempting to account for similar natural features) or mutual influence, rather than a reflection of a common historical experience.

27. E. Estyn Evans, *Irish Folk Ways* (London, 1957), passim, has demonstrated the survival to modern times in Ireland of many Neolithic tools and practices. Much of Irish folk culture was typical of the oceanic fringes of Europe until quite recently (cf. pp. 1–12); hence, his arguments can be applied to Breton culture as well.

28. Bromwich, "Cantre'r Gwaelod," pp. 240–41, has pointed out that the historical attributions of Welsh and Breton stories of submersion link the tales in each case to local, legendary heroes who flourished during the "heroic age" of their peoples—the era marking the foundation of national tradition and the earliest strata of native narrative.

29. The concentration of megalithic monuments in many Celtic areas may have contributed to the preservation of placelore associated with Stone Age events.

30. For stories of this sort see Gette de la Saudraye, *Soirs d'hiver en Bretagne* (Brest, 1891), pp. 23–28; H. Le Carguet, *Légendes de la ville d'Is* (Quimper, 1902?), nos. 2, 8; Anatole Le Braz, *La légende de la mort chez les Bretons armoricains*, ed. Georges Dottin, 3rd ed. (Paris, 1912), 1:383.

31. Johnson, *Folktales of Brittany*, p. 54.

32. Paul-Yves Sébillot, *Le folklore de la Bretagne* (Paris, 1968), 2: chap. 2; see especially p. 23.

33. La Borderie, *Cartulaire*, pp. 81–82 (bk. 2, chap. 19). For translations see La Borderie, *Histoire*, pp. 321–22, and La Borderie, "Gradlon-Mur," p. 831; cf. Bromwich, "Cantre'r Gwaelod," p. 239.

34. Cf. Rachel Bromwich, *Trioedd Ynys Prydein, The Welsh Triads* (Cardiff, 1961); and Kuno Meyer, *The Triads of Ireland* (Dublin, 1906).

35. Guenolé and Corentin were also probably heroes of popular tales, many of which are doubtless represented in the texts of their lives. Through the last century Guenolé continued to be the hero of a series of stories in which he and the devil try to best each other. Needless to say, Guenolé is always the victor. Le Carguet, *La ville d'Is*, nos. 3–6.

36. Cf. Bromwich, "Cantre'r Gwaelod," p. 238. In Irish literature the characterization of Finn mac Cumaill shows a similar development.

37. La Borderie, *Cartulaire*, p. 152 (charter no. 20); trans. La Borderie, *Histoire*, p. 324.

38. La Borderie, *Cartulaire*, p. 148 (charter no. 10).

39. La Borderie, *Histoire*, pp. 324–25; Bromwich, "Cantre'r Gwaelod," pp. 239–40.

40. The Carolingian monarchs play similar roles in the Old French epic cycle of Guillaume d'Orange, which was popular in the Middle Ages from the eleventh century onward.

41. Latouche, *Mélanges*, p. 8, nn. 1, 2; p. 92 ff. Bromwich, "Cantre'r Gwaelod," pp. 238–40.

42. See, for example, "The Debility of the Ulstermen," "The Adventures of Art Son of Conn," and "The Voyage of Bran," in *Ancient Irish Tales*, ed. T. P. Cross and C. H. Slover (1936; rept. ed., New York, 1969). See too the motif of surprising a supernatural woman bathing in "The Dream of Oenghus," trans. Kenneth Jackson, *A Celtic Miscellany* (London, 1951).

43. Cross and Slover, *Ancient Irish Tales*, pp. 208–10.

44. An edition of the lay with a critical introduction is found in Evie Margaret Grimes, *The Lays of Desiré, Graelant and Melion* (New York, 1928), pp. 76–101. Cf. Jeanne Lods, ed., *Les lais de Marie de France* (Paris, 1959), p. vii.

45. Le Carguet, *La ville d'Is*, no. 9.

46. Examples are found in Cross and Slover, *Ancient Irish Tales*, pp. 131–42, 360–69, and in Whitley Stokes, "Cóir Anmann, Fitness of Names," *Irische Texte mit Übersetzungen und Wörterbuch*, ed. Whitley Stokes and Ernst Windisch, 3rd series (Leipzig, 1897), 2:285–444.

47. Le Carguet, *La ville d'Is*, no. 11. Emile Souvestre, *Le foyer breton* (Paris, 1874), p. 243. Cf. Cambry's account, p. xvii.

48. Richard L. Brengle, *Arthur King of Britain* (New York, 1964), p. 6.

49. Grimes, *Lays*, pp. 101–2. Théodore Hersart de la Villemarqué, *Barzaz-Breiz, chants populaires de la Bretagne*, 4th ed. (Paris, 1846; recte 2nd ed., Paris, 1845), 1:68–69.

50. In *La tradition celtique en Bretagne armoricaine* (Paris, 1975), pp. 60–108, Jean Markale develops a similar argument. He suggests, however, that there was once a full saga dealing with all the details of Gradlon's life, of which we now have only fragmentary remains. It seems more likely that the tradition was less monolithic than Markale would have it; probably there were many oral tales circulating about Gradlon which were neither

perfectly consistent nor necessarily linked to each other systematically. Both Markale and I, however, would concur that Gradlon was a major figure in Breton tradition.

51. Rachel Bromwich, "The Welsh Triads," in *Arthurian Literature in the Middle Ages*, ed. Roger Sherman Loomis (Oxford, 1959), pp. 44–51.

52. La Borderie, "Gradlon-Mur," p. 833. Paul Sébillot, *Les souvenirs historiques et les héros populaires en Bretagne* (Vannes, 1889), p. 5.

53. La Borderie, *Histoire*, p. 323, proposes that the nucleus of the legend of Ker-Is was suggested by the end of the *Lay of Graelant*, but that the good fairy was transmuted to the evil Dahut. Since Dahut is a late development of the legend (see pp. xv ff., above), La Borderie's argument is not fully valid. However, the location of the other world under water in the *Lay of Graelant* may have helped attract the story of the submerged city to Gradlon.

54. The story of the city of Ys is not included in late fifteenth-century or early sixteenth-century texts, including Alain Bouchart's *Les grandes croniques de Bretaigne* (1514; reprint ed., Rennes, 1886), which is the first printed history of Brittany. More significantly, the story is omitted from the first draft of Pierre Le Baud's *Cronicques & ystoires des Bretons*, 4 vols. (Rennes, 1907–22), which he compiled c. 1480 (1:1). It seems likely that their silence on this point indicates that the story of the submerged city had not yet become widely received as a feature of tradition about Gradlon.

Le Baud died in 1505 (not in 1515, as reported by Ogès, "La ville d'Is," p. 83, and by Bromwich, "Cantre'r Gwaelod," p. 235). He left unpublished his second draft, prepared in 1498–1505 under the auspices of Anne of Brittany (Le Baud, *Croniques*, 1:1–2). The work was first published in 1638; the printed version does include a version of the story of Ker-Is that is rather similar to other early seventeenth-century versions (ibid., 3:43–44; see above, pp. xiv–xv). Whether the 1638 tale was found in the manuscript prepared by Le Baud, or whether (as I suspect) it was added by a later editor, I cannot say with certainty.

The relative dating of all the versions of the tale is extremely complex. Argentré's story may well be earlier than I have indicated here, since the first edition of his work appeared in 1582. As I have indicated below (note 68), however, the legend was in a period of rapid development in the sixteenth and seventeenth centuries, and it is not possible to conclude from a late copy or a late edition what the original was like. The tendency to elaborate on the legend also affects the dating of the mystery plays (see pp. xiv–xv) which contain the early Christianized version of the story.

If Le Baud himself included in his second manuscript a version of the story of Ker-Is figuring Guenolé, the Christianized version of the story is earlier than I have indicated. Even if this is so, however, the fact that the story is recounted by neither Le Baud in 1480, nor Bouchart in 1514, nor Argentré in 1588 indicates that the religious version was not widespread in literature or popular tradition until the very end of the sixteenth or the beginning of the seventeenth century.

55. Translated from the text quoted in Le Braz, *Légende de la mort*, ed. Dottin, pp. 388–89.

56. The surviving texts with commentary and criticism are found in (1) E. Ernault, ed. and trans., "L'ancien mystère de Saint Gwénolé avec traduction et notes," *Annales de Bretagne* 40 (1932–33):2–35; 41 (1934):104–41, 318–79. (2) François-Marie Luzel, ed. and trans., *Buhez Sant Gwennolé, abad; La vie de Saint Gwennolé abbé* (Quimper, 1889). (3) E. Ernault, "Sur le mystère de Saint Guénolé," *Revue celtique* 20 (1899):213–47. (4) P. Le Nestour, "*Vie de Saint Guénolé*, mystère breton en deux journées et quatre actes," *Revue celtique* 15 (1894):245–71.

57. The version edited by Ernault, "L'ancien mystère," 41:118–41, 318–37, spends 390 of the 1,279 lines in the play on the inundation of the city of Ys. Luzel, *Buhez*, pp. 125–

93, devotes two of the six acts (thirty-five pages of text) to the story of Ker-Is.

58. The explicit biblical references are found in Ernault, "L'ancien mystère," 41:124–31, 138–39, 318–19, 334–35; and Luzel, *Buhez*, pp. 175–89. In the Luzel text Gradlon, like Lot, also loses a companion, a young priest who dares to look back and is petrified as the flood washes over the city.

59. I have not seen a first edition of Albert le Grand's work, but its contents can be inferred. It is apparently similar to the version translated below, but without paragraph four of the translation. See below, note 61. Bromwich, "Cantre'r Gwaelod," p. 236 n. 1, argues that the mystery plays derive from an early edition of Albert le Grand. While this is possible, there are various archaic elements in the plays—including an almost epic emphasis on war and fighting—not found in Le Grand. I prefer to see the plays as representing a tradition that Albert le Grand appropriated.

60. The version published in 1638 under Le Baud's name (see note 54, above) is perfectly typical of the early seventeenth-century development of the tale. The version by Moreau quoted in Ogès, "La ville d'Is," p. 84, shows similar traits including the motif of dissolution and punishment. Moreau, however, represents the city as being conquered by the sea *par succession de temps,* 'in the course of time,' rather than by sudden inundation. Moreau indicates that he has oral rather than written sources for his information, and his account may indicate a blending of the earlier oral tradition with the religious motifs of the mystery plays and with Albert le Grand's version.

61. I am indebted to Bromwich, "Cantre'r Gwaelod," pp. 235–36, for this information. She indicates that the material in paragraph four of the passage quoted below is found for the first time in the third edition.

62. Various theories have been proposed to explain Dahut's introduction into the legend. Ogès, "La ville d'Is," pp. 85–86, suggests she was introduced by preachers who wished to add a striking element to a rather gloomy tale. Bromwich, "Cantre'r Gwaelod," pp. 237–38, says:

> The characteristic difference between the tale of Ker-Is and the Welsh tales lies in the ecclesiastical *milieu* in which the story has been preserved; in the reputed association between Grallon and St Guennolé. The tale became circulated with the impress given to it by Le Grand in his *Life of St. Guennolé,* and this ecclesiastical *milieu* in its turn profoundly influenced the development of the popular version. This appears in the transference of responsibility for the disaster from Grallon to his daughter Dahut, since it appeared illogical that Grallon, the friend and benefactor of the Church, should be regarded as responsible for the excesses of the wicked city.

63. Translated from Albert le Grand, *Les vies des saints de la Bretagne armorique,* ed. A–M Thomas and J–M Abgrall, 5th ed. (Quimper, 1901), p. 63.

64. Placelore is conservative and takes a long time to develop. Thus, generally, placelore attached to any given figure indicates that tales about that figure have been told in the region in question for a long time. To find placelore about Dahut in her first association with the legend of Ker-Is indicates that she was not a simple literary invention, but rather that she was probably the subject of earlier traditions assimilated in some fashion to the story of the city of Ys.

65. Translated from Cambry, *Voyage dans le Finistère,* 3 vols. (Paris, year VII of the French Republic [1799]), 2:284–87. Cambry (1749–1808) was administrator of the department of Finistere during the French Revolution. During his administration he travelled through the department noting economic, statistic, and ethnographic material. He pub-

lished the results of his observations four years later. Cambry could not speak Breton so depended on translators for his information about literary traditions. He is considered a precursor to the romantics. Cf. Francis Gourvil, *Théodore-Claude-Henri Hersart de la Villemarqué (1815–1895) et le "Barzaz-Breiz" (1839–1845–1867)* (Rennes, 1960), pp. 297–99; and Ogès, "La ville d'Is," p. 87.

66. North, *Sunken Cities*, pp. 94–98, 122, 145. The version of the Breton mystery play published by Luzel, *Buhez* (eighteenth-century redaction?) includes a scene of eating and drinking at a tavern prior to the inundation (v, ii). It is difficult to say whether the scene is a reflex of the feast motif found in Welsh tradition or whether it is a demonstration of the sin of gluttony. In Welsh tradition the feast motif is often connected with the theme of evil and vengeance; at times the protagonist of the story has committed a murder, in particular the murder of his predecessor in the kingship/lordship. We may have echoes of the same development of the story of Ys in eighteenth-century Breton chronicles that suggest Gradlon was implicated in his predecessor's death. Pierre-Hyacinth Morice, *Histoire ecclesiastique et civile de Bretagne*, 2 vols. (Paris, 1750), 1:10, reports, "He was suspected to have had a hand in his predecessor's death, and perhaps to have been the principal author of the deed" (my translation). Cf. Christophe-Paul Sire de Robien, *Description historique, topographique et naturelle de l'ancienne Armorique* (1756; reprint ed., Mayenne, 1974), p. 59. De Robien seems to follow Morice.

67. In several Welsh versions there is the motif of a single rider escaping. See Bromwich, "Cantre'r Gwaelod," pp. 217–20 (st. 7); North, *Sunken Cities*, pp. 68, 120–22, cf. 86, 94–95.

68. I have given only a brief sketch of the development of the legend during this early period, and my work parallels Ogès, "La ville d'Is." It remains to be done in detail. One of the difficulties in establishing a precise chronology is that it appears that the popularity of the legend was growing rapidly during the period in question. Hence, each time there was a new edition of a work in which the legend appeared, the material on Ys was expanded. We have already seen the change in the legend between the first and third editions of Albert le Grand.

Similarly, compare the text of Argentré's second edition (quoted above, pp. xiii–xiv) with the text of the fourth edition (recte 3rd ed., 1618?; translated from the passage quoted in Ogès, "La ville d'Is," p. 84):

> The local people maintain as tradition passed from person to person that in the olden times, before the coming of the Dukes to Quimper-Corentin, there was a large city called Is on the edge of the sea, which they say was submerged and covered, with King Grallon being in it. From which hazard he escaped miraculously. And ruins are still evident in this area. But of that there is no great evidence and the city of Is (if it existed) is not named by any ancient authority but some legends.

In this edition, then, the editor has modified the passage to indicate that Gradlon escaped miraculously (*par miracle*). Thus the passage was brought into conformity with the standard seventeenth-century account that Gradlon did not perish with Ys; presumably the allusion to a miracle is an oblique reference to Guenolé's role.

The passage was altered still again for the 1668 edition, in which the relevant line reads, "[and they say] that the king Grallon was in [the city] when it was ruined and that miraculously he was saved by the prayers of Saint Guenolé." (Translated from Bertrand d'Argentré, *L'histoire de Bretagne* [Rennes, 1668], p. 70.) Thus, Guenolé came to be mentioned quite explicitly.

These changes in Argentré's text illustrate the difficulty in concluding anything about the development of the legend based on the author's death date. Argentré died in 1590 (reported as 1580 by Ogès, "La ville d'Is," p. 84, and Bromwich, "Cantre'r Gwaelod," p. 235; but see *National Union Catalogue, Pre-1956 Imprints*, vol. 20 [London, 1969], pp. 374–75). However, his editors continued to revise his text after his death—at least insofar as the legend of Ys was concerned—and to modify it to meet the accepted tradition of their times. Thus, it is important for our conclusions to specify edition and/or date of any given work; one can conclude nothing about earlier editions from later printings (see note 54, above). To investigate the development of the legend of Ker-Is in any detail, then, one would have to have access to each edition of all of these early printed books. I have not been able to undertake the enterprise for this present work.

The seventeenth-century tendency to expand passages on the city of Ys and the freedom editors allowed themselves to do this underly my judgment that the 1638 version of the tale published under Le Baud's name (d. 1505) is not likely to be his work (cf. notes 54, 60, above).

69. Emile Souvestre (1806–54) was born in Morlaix. He began as a clerk in a bookstore in Nantes, and later was a writer for a Brest newspaper, *Le Finistère*. In this period he began publishing articles on Breton lore. In 1835 he left for Paris, taking material on Brittany with him. Thereafter he published numerous volumes of Breton stories, as well as novels, plays, and other works. He returned several times to Brittany to gather local material for his publications, some sixty volumes.

Souvestre's treatment of oral tradition was typical of many collectors of his time. Unlike a modern collector, he did not give information about his sources, nor did he provide a literal transcription of the teller's words (either in Breton or a close French translation). Rather, he merged oral information with material gleaned from literary sources, and recast the whole into a polished literary version. The tendency to rework oral material into literary forms is a defect as much as of his time as of Souvestre himself. The process, however, allowed for romanticization and thematic adaptation of the story of Ker-Is.

70. See Ogès, "La ville d'Is," pp. 87–91, for a detailed treatment of Souvestre's nineteenth-century precursors, his sources, and his own invention. Ogès treatment may be complicated, however, by Souvestre's version in *En Bretagne*, which Ogès does not discuss. That version seems to be earlier than the longer tale in *Le foyer breton*; it is simpler, contains motifs used by other authors in the third and fourth decades of the nineteenth century, and does not allude to motifs introduced in *Le foyer breton*. However, the earliest edition of *En Bretagne* that I have found is dated 1867, thirteen years after Souvestre's death. It is nonetheless possible that it appeared earlier: there are several references to events of 1836, and an allusion to only one of Souvestre's other works (*Les derniers Bretons*, 1835–36). On the other hand, one of the chapters refers to a trip undertaken in 1850, but this may represent a posthumous addition for the 1867 publication.

71. North, *Sunken Cities*, p. 154 ff., claims that the motif of dikes, dams, and sluice gates is a late addition to the Welsh legends inspired by travellers' tales of the submerged lands in Holland and the dikes built in the lowlands to protect them from the sea.

72. Translated from Emile Souvestre, *En Bretagne* (1867; reprint ed., Le Portulan, 1971), p. 7.

73. Ibid., pp. 6–8.

74. Translated from ibid., p. 6.

75. Translated from Souvestre, *Le foyer breton*, p. 236.

76. On the korigans, see Sébillot, *Folklore*, vol. 2, chap. 2, particularly p. 13; and La Saudraye, *Soirs d'hiver*, pp. 23–28.

77. Souvestre, *En Bretagne*, pp. 6, 9; Souvestre, *Le foyer breton*, p. 232.

78. North, *Sunken Cities*, p. 132.

79. Gourvil, *La Villemarqué*, pp. 106–12.

80. Translated from La Villemarqué, *Barzaz-Breiz*, 1:64–65.

81. Ibid., 1:66–67; Cf. Joseph Bédier, ed. and trans., *La Chanson de Roland*, rev. ed. (Paris, 1937), lines 115–19, 2496–2569.

82. Quoted in Gourvil, *La Villemarqué*, p. 169. Celtic material produced the same invidious comparisons in other countries.

83. See Gourvil, *La Villemarqué*, pp. 485–94. Cf. Bromwich's interesting comments on some of the elements that influenced La Villemarqué's treatment of the legend of Ker-Is ("Cantre'r Gwaelod," pp. 232–34). "La submersion de la ville d'Is" was one of the first poems by La Villemarqué to be recognized as his own creation; as early as 1867 it was noted that the song was not part of oral tradition in Brittany (Gourvil, *La Villemarqué*, pp. 190, 388).

84. See the translation by Tom Taylor, *Ballads and Songs of Brittany* (London, 1865), pp. 31–38.

85. 2nd ed. (Toulouse, 1855; 1st ed. Bordeaux, 1854), pp. 47–57.

86. Translated from ibid., pp. 50, 52.

87. See, for example, Luzel, *Buhez*, pp. 124–25, 128–29, 132–33, 138–39, 162–65, 168–69.

88. I have not been able to examine Souêtre's song myself. For the information in this paragraph I am indebted to Gourvil, *La Villemarqué*, p. 142; Ogès, "La ville d'Is," p. 91; and Markale, *Tradition celtique*, p. 103 n. 1.

89. Gourvil, *La Villemarqué*, p. 65 n. 2.

90. Ogès, "La ville d'Is," p. 85 n. 3, dates the painting between 1840 and 1850, a period of peak interest in the legend, when several literary versions were produced.

91. For example, the gulf where the bodies of Dahut's lovers are disposed is in the sea, not inland near Carhaix as Souvestre would have it (Souvestre, *En Bretagne*, p. 7; *Le foyer breton*, p. 238; cf. Ogès, "La ville d'Is," pp. 86–90). Similarly, Dahut's satanic lover becomes a rival of the sea in Guyot's development of the tale; the sea is presented in a personified and animistic mode, rather than as an inanimate vehicle of God's vengeance or as an impersonal, dangerous force.

92. See p. 37, below, where the reference to Teutates follows Le Breton de la Haize, *Moeurs*, p. 51, and Souêtre's song discussed on p. xxii. The account of Dahut's theft of her father's keys on p. 81 ff. is an adaptation of sections 2 and 3 of La Villemarqué's poem (*Barzaz-Breiz*, 1:64–67). Guenolé's prophesy on p. 63 is also derived from La Villemarqué (cf. p. xxi, above).

93. In his use of the saints' lives, Guyot follows Souvestre, *En Bretagne*, pp. 3–8, which includes the tales relating to Corentin and Guenolé. Guyot's material on the Senes is ultimately an adaptation of information contained in a first-century geographical tract by Pomponius Mela (*De situ orbis libri III*, book 2, chap. 6).

94. Morvark, Gradlon's horse, and Malgven, Gradlon's lover and Dahut's mother, are two of Guyot's additions. Cf. Ogès, "La ville d'Is," p. 91.

95. Ogès gives the same judgment. He says that many episodes "are not, as one might think, the work of the people but of churchmen. . . . These additions were later adopted by the people who transmitted them to later generations." He reiterates, "The role of the people in the development of the legend of the city of Is appears to be almost nil. They were only the agent of transmission that in some way incorporated the inventions of ecclesiastics and writers." Translated from ibid., pp. 83, 91.

North, *Sunken Cities*, is of the same opinion about the development of the Welsh legends of submersion. He states, "The impression created by a comparative study of our ancient legends is that in their present forms many of them owe more to educated authors than to simple country folk—more to journalism than to tradition. . . . Whatever part the common folk . . . may have played in preserving the germ of the story, it is to educated writers that we owe its elaboration and its survival. . . . One cannot help feeling that, in most cases, the legends actually current amongst the country folk, before modern authors began to 'write them up,' were simple tales with a minimum of circumstantial detail . . ." (pp. 14, 87, 145). Cf. note 60 and the discussion of Souêtre's song on p. xxii.

96. Le Carguet, *La ville d'Is*, nos. 1, 2, 10. Le Braz, *Légende de la mort*, pp. 381–88.

97. Translated from ibid., p. 385.

98. Translated from ibid., p. 383.

99. References to crystal are common in descriptions of the Celtic other world. See, for example, Cross and Slover, *Ancient Irish Tales*, pp. 490, 494, 589; Whitley Stokes, "The Voyage of the Húi Corra," *Revue celtique* 14 (1893):58–59. Summaries of accounts of the Celtic other world are found in Patch, *The Otherworld*, pp. 27–59.

100. Le Carguet, *La ville d'Is*, no. 1, and also p. 33 where there appears to be a piece of rationalization invented by either Le Carguet or one of his informants: "The locks that protected the city against the sea numbered twelve. The largest, called 'The Well' (*Puits*), which was opened by Ahès, was located at Gorlé-Gréis" (my translation).

La Villemarqué, *Barzaz-Breiz*, 1:63, also refers to a "well" (*puits*) or "immense basin" which protected the city from the sea. It is impossible to tell whether he learned this tradition from an informant or whether he was inspired to add it by his knowledge of Welsh literature in general and the story of Cantre'r Gwaelod in particular. Cf. Bromwich, "Cantre'r Gwaelod," pp. 232–34, where she discusses other elements in La Villemarqué's poem that show Welsh influence; and Gourvil, *La Villemarqué*, pp. 66–74.

101. Le Carguet, *La ville d'Is*, p. 33.

102. Johnson, *Folktales of Brittany*, p. 58. Johnson also likens the legend of Ker-Is to that of King Arthur whom the Bretons also believe "to be not dead but *rex futurus*" (p. 57). Both legends have assumed political overtones. Johnson points out that the earliest written record of the tale of the city of Ys occurs only a century after Brittany lost its independence through the marriage in 1491 of Anne of Brittany to Charles VIII of France. Thus, the period of growth of the legend (sixteenth to eighteenth centuries) corresponds to the period when Brittany was assimilating the fact of its lost sovereignty.

Translator's Note

Without the unflagging help and encouragement of my good friends, Jean and John Arsenian, this project would never have been realized. Thanks are also due to Dr. William Gugli, professor of French at the University of Massachusetts at Amherst, who wisely and patiently corrected my readings of Guyot's text, and to Kenneth Walker, University Editor, for his understanding and help with the style and tone of the entire work.

What I say here about the legend is a subjective opinion, an expression of how I have come to view it, how my thoughts have encompassed it and led me into it. I was drawn to the legend by its images; they enraptured and compelled me. It was as I began to turn those images into drawings that the thoughts expressed here began to articulate themselves and, in so doing, to make room for new and perhaps deeper images in a second and a third series of drawings. Images, drawings, thought—all three are interwoven.

I first heard of the legend of the city of Ys from Jacques Monteil, who is from Brittany. He spoke of a place; you fly over it, he said, and see old roads leading to the shore's edge and abruptly stopping. He said these were old roads to Ys, the city that was and is no more. He spoke of Dahut the beautiful, who for love sold the keys of the dike to the devil, and of how he opened the dike in a storm and she drowned in the flood.

I was taken with the story. Perhaps Jacques's feeling for the legend transmitted itself to me; perhaps it stirred in me some memory from another time. As a girl I had taken my troubles to the sea, and had buried my passions in the sand and salt. Perhaps this drew me to the legend; perhaps it allowed a legitimate passage to paper of long-dammed passions.

The only version of the legend I could find was Guyot's, and his is both entrancing and visually beautiful. With his retelling before me, the inadequacies of my own knowledge both of French and of that period in history were thrust out of the way, thrown aside by my passion for the story and my desire to turn it into drawings.

It began with a feeling for the place—Cornouaille, Quimper, the rocky coast of Brittany. I know Plogoff and the Isle of Sein as if they were my own, although I have never set foot upon that space of earth nor heard the sea beat upon those rocks. Perhaps I took from Jacques his love of that land and made it my own. Certainly it was he who gave me my first vision of the city and the legend. But as I entered into the legend more deeply, I left the place behind, and came to see it increasingly as an account of the struggle between pagan and Christian.

Guyot dates the legend from the fifth century. It seems to me that at that time the struggle between Christian and pagan for the land, for power, and for the faith of the people would have had some fierceness to it. Perhaps an older legend about a lost city was picked up and made a Christian legend, meant to reflect the struggle between the old gods and the new religion, meant to show the strength and goodness of the one and the evil and wickedness of the other. Certainly Guyot's version reflects that struggle; moreover, in his version there is a clear split between men and women, and it is the women who are the antagonists. From somewhere I have an image of Celtic women as more fierce and independent than their Greek and Roman counterparts. And this fierceness and independence threatened the Church, which felt a need to do battle against such women, to hammer them into shape or submission. Some say the Korrigans were pagan princesses of Brittany who refused to submit to Christianity and retreated to the forest. Perhaps what was taking place was that as the old beliefs in the power of women broke down, women became more vulnerable in the swiftly changing society of those years; the Church offered them protection at the price of submitting to its rule and subjecting a part of themselves.

Beyond both the place itself and the pagan-Christian conflict, I came to read the legend on a somewhat symbolic level, not only as a legend but almost as a myth. Its mythological beginnings concern a woman's experience, the struggle of a passionate and strong-willed woman to understand herself and her sexuality and at the same time to resist the demands of the world that she conform. And with this positive struggle, there seems to run through the cloth of the story another thread: that of fearing women, their power, and their supposed wicked use of that power.

It purports to be a legend about a wicked woman, but as Dahut came alive for me, her wickedness wore thin. I began to look more closely at how she had been drawn and why, and came to love her strengths and know her struggle. It was a struggle to coexist with her own power and passion, and to be loved without relinquishing either. And she lost on all grounds.

I still find all that in the story, but of late I have come to view it less narrowly, to see more of its whole human dimension. As I translated Guyot, my complete focus was on Dahut, Malgven, Keban, and the priestesses of the Isle of Sein. I was their champion; Corentin, Ronan, Guenolé were my enemies; Gradlon I forgave because he loved Dahut so well, or at least so much. Now, as I have gained some distance, my view has rounded. I love Dahut no less, but I see more clearly how each character in the legend has a hand in what happens. For me, the legend of the city of Ys was a beautiful gift, containing as it does the essence of all great literature—the power to stir life, to light fires, to kindle dreams.

D. C.

The Bereavement of Gradlon

IN THE CHATEAU OF QUIMPER, in great bereavement and in great sadness, lived Gradlon, king of Cornouaille. All through the day in his innermost chamber, far from the light, he lay on his bed speaking only to ask his servant for drink. And if he did not drink, he slept.

His best men were weary of this. They suffered and grumbled, and sometimes they gently took him to task:

"Lord, sadness and shame you have given us. No one sees you any longer leaving in grand procession for war or for the hunt. Yet who knows better than you how to wield the sword or pull the huntsman's bow? Who knows better how to wait out the wild boar, or to follow the track of the stag? Alas, the people of Leon, who are our subjects, say under their breath that the sword-arm of Cornouaille has become feeble; and those of Vanne, who are our rivals, say it loudly. Know also, lord, that in the country of the Gallois they declare the time has come to seize the beautiful city of Quimper. At such remarks, our hearts beat with anger and the blood rises in our faces. Lord, do you not feel these speakers of evil should be punished?"

But Gradlon, without a word in answer, called for his cup-bearer and held out to him his goblet of gold.

"Lord king," pursued his courtiers heatedly, "if you will not bid us to battle, nor conduct us on the hunt, then name one of us, by favor, to stand in your place. He will be your man and our chief; and as we are to you, we each will be faithful to him. Nothing is accomplished by leaving the sword in the sheath and the war horse in the pasture. A rusty sword and a fattened horse are no longer good at war."

"My sons," Gradlon then said, "leave me in peace, I pray you. Neither combats nor hunts suit me at this moment; and if one of you wishes to put himself in my place, let him try. He will know then if the lord of Cornouaille has a feeble arm."

And if they persisted, he threatened them with death, because he was drunk, angry, and in a black humor.

Failing thus in their purpose, the courtiers brought from Aquitaine some skillful performers of poem and song; jugglers, rope dancers, mimics, face-makers, and animal trainers. "Sire," they said, "we shall lift you out of your grief. See these games and diversions, hear these beautiful poems. They will chase away your ennui as the sun does the clouds."

And the players and jugglers, the mimics and face-makers, tried their best. No one was able to hear them without being moved by their sweet songs, nor see their good tricks without a hearty laugh.

Gradlon alone turned away from them. Instead of the money and gifts they had received elsewhere, he dismissed them harshly; they were happy to avoid the noose.

If the king of Cornouaille thus repulsed friends and pleasure, it was because of the sadness, soul and body, he suffered without rest. Some days the walls of the palace trembled from the howling of his voice, like that of the wild beasts of the forest. He knocked the walls with his fists and with his head. He wrecked the very chairs around him. The silence of the night was shattered with horrible sounds. All fled his madness and hid themselves in great fear.

These things had all come to pass since Queen Malgven had died.

In these moments there was only one man capable of quieting the king, of calming his terrible fury. This was an old poet, white of hair and beard, honored for his knowledge and the majesty of his songs. He played his harp in such a style, he sang with such sensitivity that no one could hear him without crying softly if he put sadness into his melodies, or without sharing in great courage and comfort if he sang of high deeds and prowess. Gradlon held this singer in friendship, often sending for him and imploring him to sing the Lay of Gradlon's Love.

Now the lay was such as this, and the old poet recited it in a powerful voice as his fingers moved over the two strings of his harp, one deep as the somber wood from which the harp was made, the other biting and burning as its decorations of gold:

King Gradlon prepares to wage war
far in the North, such is his challenging task.
There are cities, chateaux, walled towns and market towns,
well defended by ramparts and towers.

There, too, are granaries and beautiful treasures,
glory and plunder, demanding of danger and death.

Hard is the wind, large the green ocean,
long the way to these countries of winter.
Everywhere reefs, shipwrecks and storms,
to the sailor promising want and pain.
How many leave never to return to their land,
put to sleep in the tomb of the sea.

Gradlon the king summoned all his people
to assist him in battle and with money,
rigged out his ships and unfurled his sail,
took his sword and his hauberk of mail;
left the port of beautiful days
untouched by storms.
One hundred beautiful ships sailed in his wake.

Thus sang the old poet, and Gradlon saw again the grey sky of the North, the
mornings without laughter and the boredom that came with the cold and the
calm weather, when the sails flapped and the sailors in great discomfort
shivered in the depths of the ship.

The singer told of these troubles and struggles; he recalled the far-off
shores, the remote cities appearing suddenly through the mist and as quickly
effaced. He sang:

At the fiord's edge is an ancient city
enclosed by ramparts, full of famous donjons.
Upon the rocks her fortress walls are fixed;
the fierce sea breaks at her beach.
In her houses is wealth of every sort;
two thousand stalwarts defend the gates.

There came Gradlon through winds and storms,
one hundred beautiful vessels sailing in his wake.
He saw the beach and the city well enclosed,
and the rocks where the waves broke.
Then smiling at ease and in good hope:
"Friends," he said, "we shall take it tonight!"

But neither ruse nor force took it.
High were the walls and solid the gates.
For two months he pressed and besieged them.
The surrounding mountains have their cloaks of snow.

"Soon comes the winter," murmured the barons.

"What folly! Alas, we shall all die here."

But Gradlon no longer heard the old singer. With his eyes closed he saw again the inaccessible city set on the high rock at the foot of the snow-covered mountains. And on the stony beach he saw, white and frail, the tents of Cornouaille pressed in by the sea. And he heard again the voices of his men:

"King Gradlon, foolishness is not virtue. How many have fallen already on this beach? Persist no longer. Do you wish us to perish from cold and worry? Return to Cornouaille! There the winter is sweet, new wine fills the cellars. Sadly our wives look to the sea, praying it will soon bring again our white sails."

He rebuked them, calling them cowards and faithless, but as soon as the wind blew from the south they pushed their ships to the water.

"Embark, King Gradlon, the breeze already pushes us!"

"I will leave only when I have taken the city, killed its prince and conquered its treasure."

"Will you take it alone, King Gradlon?"

"Alone I shall take it, if alone I remain."

"Then God and His saints keep you."

They laughed loudly, and jumped on board. Soon they sailed away by grace of the prompt wind. Gradlon was left on the beach without a companion. He heard his heart speak, saying:

"Remain; a thousand swords are not worth one strong arm, a thousand cowards do not equal one brave man."

The darkness came down. That evening and every evening he went around the high wall, seeking a secret entrance, a badly closed gap, a sleeping guard.

Now by the turn of the moat, a great surprise awaited him. A few steps away in front of a tower stood a motionless form. And Gradlon saw that it was a woman, by the golden hair which covered her shoulders and flowed the length of her figure. From all other signs he would have taken her for a soldier. She wore armor of blue steel, a corslet of heavy mail; her right hand rested on a shield and at her side hung a large sword. But when the moon swam out from the clouds and enveloped her in its slanting light Gradlon saw her beautiful arms, white and round, naked outside the hauberk. Her eyes ashen, her breast swelling under the iron, she appeared both terrible and charming in the moonlight. Majestic and tranquil her face; on her forehead gleamed a diadem of gold, at her waist was a golden ribbon, and red rubies shone upon her breast.

From fear trembled Gradlon the strong; with desire quivered Gradlon the wise. Without sound he walked in the shadows; she heard him nonetheless, this strange warrior. A light and mysterious voice pierced the silence:

"Approach. I know who you are: he who each night, when all but the watchers sleep, prowls around us as a bad spirit or as a wild beast come down from the mountains. You are he who has searched each inch of this soil, tested each stone, measured the height of each citadel. Good is this enclosure. The gates defy the battering ram, the towers defy scaling. Stranger, what are you seeking on this shore?"

Gradlon had pulled back into the shadow, through prudence and fear of ambush. But all around was only the smooth wall, the exposed rock, nothing which could hide a trap. He advanced into the circle of moonlight, saying:

"Who are you?"

"Yourself, tell me your name, if it is of a loyal man and a courageous chief."

"I am Gradlon, king of Cornouaille. I have one hundred ships on the sea. I have three thousand warriors under my tents." Thus spoke Gradlon, bravely.

"What do you wish, you of Cornouaille?"

"To conquer the city, should it take ten years, and I shall do it or die here."

But under the moon amidst her pale hair, the armed woman smiled.

"Where is your force, Gradlon? Where are your ships? I have seen the men pulling up their tents. I have seen your hundred sails slipping off on the sea. The shore is empty save the place where your dead are buried."

Gradlon bowed his head:

"It is true. The cowards have fled from the discomfort and fury of the winter."

"You are here alone, then. You will not take the city, and you will die here according to your word if no miracle occurs. Is that not so?"

"Woman, miracles happen every day. At these gates I have broken my battering ram, at these walls I have planted my ladders in vain. I have felt the arrows of the defenders in my flesh, and by the hundreds my men have bitten the earth. It matters not."

"Why, Gradlon of Cornouaille, did you not listen to your men? If you had you would now be travelling toward your own kingdom at your ease."

"Woman, whoever you are, I will tell you what holds me here. A voice in my heart spoke out; I do not understand it, yet I obey it. It said: 'Remain; a thousand swords are not worth one strong arm, a thousand cowards do not equal one brave man.'"

The woman walked toward him and gently touched him on the breast.

"I am called Malgven, queen of the North; the city is mine, this country is subject to me. In my palace is my odious husband. He loves only the table and the servants' beds. At his side sleeps his useless sword. It is I, Gradlon, you have been fighting, not he. It is I who have broken your battle, murdered your brave men, stripped courage from all except you. I have seen you in the assault, terrible as a great bear; I have seen you in council, wise and dignified as an elder. And looking at you I have felt that I was a prisoner of love. Yourself, Gradlon, alone on this shore, you are a prisoner of love. Through right or through witchcraft, Gradlon, we must love."

At these words, she embraced him and kissed him on the lips, such a kiss that he trembled to the depth of his being. He staggered as if drunk. Clasping his hand she said:

"From this moment, you are mine and I am yours for always. If you wish to follow me we shall kill my husband, take his treasure, and we then shall go to your palace in Cornouaille."

She pushed a low door hidden in the wall and led him through secret ways to the palace which stood above the city. She showed him a room and a man sleeping on a rug of purple, and pulling out her own sword she handed it to Gradlon. She spoke one word:

"Strike!"

He struck the sleeper in the neck; the blood gushed out and the purple rug drank it. They took a gold coffer filled with jewels from a hiding place. Gradlon asked:

"How shall we now escape? How shall we gain my land of Cornouaille? My ships are far away. There is not a ship in your port, not one seaworthy boat remains."

Malgven replied: "I have a living ship: an enchanted horse who can carry us over the waves to your fleeing ships."

In the stable Gradlon found a stallion, black as night, without bridle or bit. The breath of his nostrils was a red vapor, flames shot from his eyes.

"No one but I can mount him," said Malgven. "The best horsemen he has thrown to death. He accepts only my hand and the name I have given him."

She called: "Morvark!"

The horse turned his flaming eyes toward her and came, docile, to her voice:

"Morvark, this is the master I have chosen. Take us over the sea to his ships. You are more rapid than the wind, you laugh at the waves, you outstrip the storms, the sea eagle wears out his tireless wings pursuing you."

Gradlon leaped onto the horse, holding the golden coffer; Malgven mounted with him. The black stallion leaped, without bridle or bit, as easily

over the ramparts as over a hedge. He galloped to the beach and flew over the foaming ocean.

And then Malgven pronounced these magic words:

"Waves, be still! Wind, cease your blowing! Oh sea, be as a path of grass under the steps of this horse of the night. He has come out of your depths to carry the burden of love. Know him, oh sea. Be kind, be sure, be merciful."

These words again echoed in the ears of Gradlon, while near him sang the poet:

> Hear, lords, that which Gradlon conquered
> in the city far away which he besieged,
> lured on by pleasure and the quest for booty;
> a woman with beautiful hair of pure gold,
> a horse more black than Lucifer,
> nostrils smoking like the gates of Hell.
>
> A greater prize he took in these two treasures
> than all the jewels, gems and golden vases.
> But on the sea blew a jealous wind,
> from coast to coast wandered King Gradlon,
> searching for his land, weeping for his domain.
> In sorrow his ships sailed for a whole year.
>
> During this year, on this ship in torment,
> the fate of love united these two lovers.
> To their great joy a child was given them,
> born amid the spray and the storm.
> The beautiful wife is dead in childbirth,
> alas, never to see the port of Cornouaille.
>
> Think, lords, after such misery,
> how Gradlon returned at last to his land,
> having under him the black steed, so proud,
> within his arms the child come from the sea,
> within his heart eternal grief and tears.
> Misery and pain are the lot of mortals.

Gradlon filled the end of the song with his own tears. He gave largess to the poet and dismissed him with kindness, saying:

"You soothe my troubles as the waves in my days of adventure soothed my ship. Then I had at my side her whom I have lost. Now I am alone and forever sad because I am eternally tied by the bonds of love. You sing the Lay of Gradlon and understand my grief, but everyone else takes me for a fool.

THE BEREAVEMENT OF GRADLON 9

And they are right if it is folly to love not just for this life but for the other."

Despite his sadness he called for them to bring him his daughter, the child from the sea. She had been given the name Dahut. She grew freely, wild and beautiful.

Gradlon held her there between his knees and looked at her eagerly. Like her mother she was fair, but of a fairness more tawny and wild, as the rays of a fire. She had Malgven's noble, imperious face, but her flesh was paler, her brow more haughty. Her eyes had the color of the changing sea, now light and calm, now dark and ominous. When moved her eyes would flash suddenly as lightning flashes out from beneath the clouds of a storm.

As Gradlon contemplates her, he says:

"Child, you give me great joy and cruel pain. No other face in the world is able to recall to me more faithfully Malgven, your mother, who died in my arms on the ocean. I desire and dread to see you because your face, the image of my dead beloved, is at the same instant a source of grief and a source of joy."

"Father," Dahut demanded, "tell me again of the Queen Malgven who died in your arms on the Ocean and whom I resemble so much."

"She was the most beautiful of women when life colored her features, yet when her eyes were closed forever she became so beautiful there is no word to describe her. You, my Dahut, my dear daughter, resemble your mother dead more than your mother living because there is something in you that is not of this earth."

"Tell me again, lord, how Malgven, your queen, was adorned on the day you gave her to the sea."

"I put on her brow a diadem of gold. I dressed her in armor of blue steel. In a corslet of fine mail I enclosed her breast, a shield covered her legs, and her sword belt hung from her waist. She seemed a sleeping Valkyrie as depicted in the Songs of the North. I kissed her with burning lips, and from that moment was hollowed out the furrow from which flow these inexhaustible tears. The sea received her beautiful body as gently as a green lawn, and the waves scattered over her their white foam as the flowers of the fields."

At this story the immense eyes of Dahut flashed, her nostrils fluttered, and her heart beat desperately.

"Father, father, as your queen, Malgven, I would die in the sea."

And King Gradlon would press her almost to the point of pain against his breast.

"Be quiet, daughter of my desire. Be quiet, my white pearl, my bird of the North."

And he smothered the ardent cries of Dahut under his kisses.

Sometimes, however, he dismissed her rudely, and in renewed despair, he gnawed and tore the covers of his bed, howling in the darkness like a wolf with a mortal wound.

The Miracle of Ronan

IN THESE TIMES, THEN, Gradlon neglected his duty as king, seldom holding assemblies, no longer rendering justice. In his place the judges bent their decisions to their pleasure and as they were slack and greedy they gave the right to the strong and oppressed the poor.

One day there entered into Quimper a peasant woman with dirty clothes and haggard eyes, her hair disheveled. She went through the streets and into the square with staggering steps crying like a madwoman:

"Justice! Justice, King Gradlon!"

The people gathered about her in the streets and said to her:

"If you truly want justice, don't tarry further. Go home, because there is no justice in Quimper."

She did not listen to them, but ran madly from house to house, banging on the doors with feet and fists, her lament and cry always:

"King Gradlon, justice!"

Then they led her to the magistrate seated in his court among the petitioners. She looked at the judge and asked him:

"Are you Gradlon?"

"I am not he. But in his name I hold the scales and the sword. Speak then before me."

But she left the court at his answer and made her way, still calling loudly on the king, putting the city in turmoil. A great crowd surrounded her now, not knowing why she made so great a noise, but demanding for her pity and justice.

When Gradlon heard the turmoil and was told the reason for it he said:

"Drive this woman out with the whip."

They did so. Nevertheless each morning she came again to the palace in spite of the guards and the watchmen, suffering blows from the pike and the lash, and pleading for justice with such fervor that in the end Gradlon decided to see her. He asked her name and whence she came.

"I am Keban. I live north of the forest of Nevelt. King Gradlon, I beg you, give me justice."

"Woman, who has done you wrong?"

"Lord, he who has done me wrong is Ronan, the hermit of the forest."

"Of what do you accuse him?"

"He has sold himself to the devil, who changes him into a wolf at nightfall."

"Woman, these are grave words. Where are your proofs?"

"King Gradlon, I had a child, a small daughter, laughing, sweet, scarcely three years old. Ronan in the shape of a wolf took her from my cabin while I was in the woods, and devoured her."

Saying this Keban fell on her knees, crying and pleading.

Gradlon himself was moved. He said in a milder voice:

"Woman, the man whom you accuse is held wise and holy by all. He lives in solitude and poverty as a wise recluse. Your words are but madness."

"King Gradlon, I saw him, I say, enter into his home in the form of a man and leave it as a wolf. In that there must be some magic, some sacrilegious pact. By God, I swear that my daughter was abducted by him and I require you to give me prompt and full justice."

"He will be judged, Keban."

"Lord, that is not all. I also accuse this Ronan, through secret and evil rites, of changing my husband who is a simple and naive man. He is a woodcutter by trade, king, and this damnable Ronan persuaded him to build his hermitage; then, to my misfortune, he kept him. Since that time I no longer have bread. I eat the berries of the bushes, the grasses which God meant for animals—not for the creatures made in His image. And I shall soon die if you do not give me reparation for my grief, if you do not avenge me against this wicked sorcerer."

"You will be avenged, woman, if the truth is in your mouth," said Gradlon. "But, it is necessary to hear the recluse, who until now has been well thought of, has led a good life, and never has broken any of our laws."

"He does not honor your laws, O king. In front of me he has slandered all kings and yourself, lord."

"Someone go to his hermitage and fetch him quickly," ordered Gradlon.

The soldiers went to the forest of Nevelt, where they surprised Ronan in his solitude. Dressed in the skin of a goat, girded with boughs, the hermit was praying at the foot of a cross.

The men of Gradlon seized him, chained him and, having conducted him to their master, they gave a report of their mission:

"We found him praying in the forest. The birds kept silent around his thatched cottage. At his side were sleeping the timid doe and the wild boar. He did not resist us. He begged us only to let him finish his prayer, as the service of God came before all your laws."

Completely amazed, the king said to Ronan:

"This Keban has accused you of sorcery. She has declared that you devour children and suborn men to your will through conjury."

Ronan replied: "I flee the society of men and live only with God. That is why I left the isle of Ireland where I was born, wishing to instruct myself in the Holy Scriptures and to live in piety. God sent me to the country of Armorica where I could love and serve Him best. What can anyone say against me? For clothes I have only the skins of beasts; a twisted branch is my belt. I drink the black water of the mire, I nourish myself with bread baked in ashes. My life is filled with prayer and penance. But, without a doubt, I am as yet unworthy to love and serve God since he has not yielded to my desire to be forgotten and forsaken by the world."

"King," cried out Keban, "close your ears to the words of this rascal. I have seen him in the guise of a wolf, slinking and howling in the forest."

"It has been reported to me," said the king to Ronan, "that for acts of magic you were driven from the country of Leon, and threatened with burning."

"It was to the country of Leon," said the hermit, "that God first called me. I built a thatched cottage and lived there a long time without any commerce with humans. Great was my joy, complete my happiness. I had only the sky above for my consolation. I devoted myself only to prayer and the practice of the Holy Laws of God. But God tested me: he placed on my path a leper who so moved me that I begged God in His almighty power to cure his miserable sores. And immediately the leper became clean of body. Then from all parts came running the sick, the infirm, the crippled, the fever-ridden, and the dying; my retreat was full of cries of pain, of hope, of relief, because the Most High, blessed be His name, as soon as I invoked Him, cleansed the wounded ones, gave to others sight, straightened up backs, limbs, brought the dying up from their stretchers. Thus the Lord of Heaven struck me, thus the sweet joys of solitude and of silence were taken from me. I was afraid then that in repairing the health of others I would lose that of my own soul, so I escaped into Cornouaille, in the forest of Nevelt, where I asked God to take me into His grace."

In spite of this, the woman Keban spat in his face, vomiting out insults:

"You pig, tormentor of souls, harbinger of Hell! Each of your words is a lie. Serpent, hangman, infamous one! You seduced my husband by witch-craft so that he left his home, his wife and his work. But he was a good companion, strong of arm; with him never did we lack for bread."

Ronan responded: "It is true that one morning a wolf sprang from the woods holding a baby in his mouth and following him came a man out of breath who cried with sadness. I was cleft to the heart by his sorrow, and for him I invoked my sovereign Lord. 'God,' I pleaded, 'let not this baby be hurt.' No sooner had I said this than the baby was put down unharmed on my threshold, at the feet of the poor serf. The man embraced my knees and I lifted him up and kissed him. He offered to help build my cabin and my chapel, and I have not dismissed him because he has a pure heart. Innocence and goodness are in him. But I have not kept him by force or through malice. Perhaps in His wisdom God has commanded that this woodcutter be my friend and advance with me in the ways of perfection."

"Will not somebody kill him with rods?" cried Keban. "Will not some-body pull out his forked tongue? He has slandered you, Gradlon, teaching that homage is not due to the kings of this earth."

And Gradlon said to the hermit:

"You are not yet vindicated."

Ronan asked: "How may I do so if God does not enlighten you?"

The king grew red with anger.

"Keban has spoken against you. What is your defense for that which you assert about the kings of the earth?"

"I have not spoken evil of the kings of the earth, no more than of you, Gradlon. I teach that only to the King immortal and invisible, to God alone, belong homage and glory."

Gradlon was displeased, and upbraided Ronan.

"These are cunning words, clever evasions. Why should we not believe that you have healed the sick, or that the spirit of God is in you? But have you forgotten that you are settled on my land and that your fate is in my hands?"

The man of God answered:

"My life belongs to the Lord of my days, my eternal master. My fate is in His hands, not in yours."

"Well," cried Gradlon, "then let Him save you."

And he said to his servants, "I have two furious mastiffs, two savage and hungry dogs. Release them upon him. They will serve as my judgment."

They took Ronan to the middle of a meadow through which ran a brook amid new flowers. They tied him there to the largest tree, and loosed Gradlon's dogs. Immediately the mastiffs darted forth to tear Ronan apart, but as they touched him the hermit made the sign of the cross on his heart saying, "May the Lord stop you."

The ferocious beasts stopped, suddenly calmed, and like peaceful lambs, went to drink at the brook.

The people clapped their hands and knelt down crying:

"Noel, Noel."

Gradlon, who was moved and contrite, himself broke the bands which held Ronan the hermit to the tree, and said to him:

"What do you wish of me, now that God has judged?"

Said Ronan: "Nothing, save to wish pardon for the woman, Keban."

The king summoned the woman and said,

"Go and thank him whom you have persecuted. Were it not for him I would have thrown you on the pyre."

But Ronan added:

"The child of Keban was neither devoured nor abducted. She hid herself in the woodbox so that you thought she had disappeared. Visit her dwelling place and open the box, and you will find her there."

They ran to the house of Keban. The little girl was in the box, stretched out on her side. She was dead there, suffocated. Then Ronan took her in his arms and called her three times, resurrecting her in the name of the Father and the Son and the Holy Spirit.

The Holy Man Corentin

THE MIRACLES OF RONAN had drawn King Gradlon up from his depression. He did not cease to drink, nor to cry for Malgven, his dear wife. But his taste for riding, for hunting, and for the games of arms returned.

A vast forest extended to the foot of the Menez-hom. Its depths were a shelter to wild animals, and Gradlon went there frequently to hunt. He sought an ease to his fever in the fatigue and noise of the chase for wild boar or stag, as futilely as he had sought it in idleness and silence.

One day, following the trails of these animals over valleys and hills through the forest, he became lost. For many hours the chase moved from clearing to clearing never finding a trail. The exhausted horses began to trip and more than one fell. Seeing this the king said:

"Gentlemen, let us stop and give our mounts time to breathe. It is not late; before evening we shall find our path."

A page advanced: "Lord, I see a cabin through the forest. It must be a woodcutter's house. Let us reach it and take council there."

Gradlon and his companions walked to the cabin and they discovered there a hermit, building a rustic altar. The king pushed toward him.

"Good hermit, tell us the shortest way to leave this forest."

"Lord," responded the man, "the forest is vast, and the edge is a long journey away for horses as heated as yours."

"We shall rest here and then you will show us the path."

"Be welcome, King Gradlon, with your people."

The king made a gesture of astonishment.

"From where do you know me? This is truly a marvel."

"Lord, king, those of God know all that God wishes them to know."

"Who are you?"

"I am Corentin, the humble servant of Jesus and Our Lady."

At this name Gradlon was gladdened: "Holy man Corentin," he said, "be well revered and venerated by me. Your virtues are truly illustrious, your renown is great. Praised be the Most High who has led me to your dwelling."

"Praised be He," said also Corentin, "because nothing comes without His wishing. Only His order is done. It is not without purpose that He has allowed your hunt to stray, King Gradlon."

Then the king seated himself near the hermit on the trunk of a fallen tree and they talked together. The king's admiration for the hermit increased, as Corentin talked of the things of the world and the things of God. He spoke simply and wisely of the one and the other.

However the king's followers, seeing him occupied with the monk and little concerned with anything else, looked at each other sadly and said:

"Shall we not eat before night, shall we have for dinner only our paternosters and prayers? They are a meager repast for men who have been hunting since dawn."

Seeing the huntsmen talking together, Corentin turned his clear look on them and with the gift which he held from God he understood what was bothering them.

"Lord king," he said to Gradlon, "the body must not suffer while the soul takes delight. God remits to our keeping the needy flesh. If one is not an unworthy servant, one should treat the body generously with his bounty. Would it not then be pleasant, after so hard a ride, to be cared for and refreshed?"

"That I would willingly," laughed the king, "because since the cock crowed I have not eaten the least morsel nor drunk the slightest drop."

"Then," said Corentin, "order your cook and your steward to get to work, so that you may not regret that you visited this poor hermit."

Gradlon called up his servants and the holy man begged them to prepare a meal.

"Long fasts are not good for soldiers," said the hermit. "Let the roasts be plentiful and the wine fresh. Thus shall you please your master and thus content God who made you His."

But the steward and the cook answered, "Sir monk, how shall we be able to please our master since we are without provisions of any sort?"

"Do we not have here enough to nourish one hundred men?" the monk said severely. "Must you learn your craft from me?"

"Sir monk," replied the steward, "we know our craft which is to prepare anywhere a good table for our master. For this we carry with us flat table service and vessels of precious metal, fit to set a table for the king of Cornouaille. But what are we to do if there is nothing to put in the vessels of gold, nothing to pour into the flasks? A recluse does not give out noble roasts nor good wine that is fit for the repast of a prince. Water is their drink, or they blend concoctions of wild herbs, bitter and odorous, or the juice of sour apples."

"And they eat only," added the cook, "barley bread and boiled roots. That is not for the mouth of King Gradlon. We shall be shamed and lost, sir monk, if we fail our king in this."

Corentin, who had listened with impatience, said to the steward:

"Bring your most copious flask."

And to the cook: "Bring your largest basket."

The steward and the cook brought, the first a golden pitcher, the second, a golden basket, the marks of their trade, and Corentin made a sign for them to follow him. They walked behind him saying softly:

"This man is mad, really. He has nothing, yet intends to nourish the king and twenty starving knights."

The good hermit led them to a spring which poured forth its clear trickle into a pool between two mossy rocks. In the transparent water frisked about a small fish, brilliant as a polished coin, rapid as an arrow. Corentin said to the steward:

"Give me your flask, sir."

He plunged the pitcher into the spring and pulled it out full of water, limpid and icy. Then turning toward the cook, he said:

"Sir, give me your basket."

And plunging his arm into the pool he caught the little fish. He cut it in two, then threw one piece into the basket and returned the other to the pool. And he said to the king's astonished officers,

"There are your provisions. My friends, under this oak tree, which God made equal to a chateau in greenery, more majestic than the arch of a palace, lay the table of the king of Cornouaille, and all his men will soon be able to satisfy their appetite."

On hearing these words the steward and the cook burst out laughing.

"Lord hermit, a humorous fantasy indeed! You want us to satisfy our thirst from a flask of pure water and to fill ourselves with part of a small fish. This can only be a monkish joke. We would enjoy it more if we did not have an empty stomach and a dry throat."

"Follow my advice," responded Corentin.

But they became angry.

"Are we beggars to be treated so? Are we frogs who must drink clear water, stray dogs to munch on fish bones?"

Corentin looked at them severely: "Faithless people, obey and God will see to what you desire."

Then with derision they gave in to his fancy; under the oak they set the royal table and covered it with dishes of gold until it seemed ready for a feast. In the middle they arranged the basket with the piece of the little fish and the flagon of clear water. This done, they went to the king with a great show of mock satisfaction.

"Sire, your repast awaits under the oak for your good pleasure."

"I am glad of that," said the king. "I feel a furious hunger and I am ready to do honor to the provisions of the holy man. What then shall I eat?"

"Lord, the holy man has given us something to accommodate you with dignity."

"But what?"

"Know then, the lower part of a small fish which swam in the fountain, a flagon of water from the stream."

All the assembly laughed and cried:

"What folly, what folly!"

Gradlon knitted his eyebrows and his look stopped their laughter.

"It displeases me," he said, "that you ridicule the holy hermit. Better valued are the good deeds of the poor than the charity of the rich."

"Lord," said Corentin, smiling, "let them cry, 'What folly,' because those of us here are foolish, in truth, who doubt the power and the goodness of God."

"Let it not be me then," said the king gayly. "I shall eat with good grace, holy man, this good cooking."

And he went toward the table set under the oak and all went with him. Suddenly a cry of amazement escaped from them all. The table was covered with delicious things most pleasing to see: pâtés, roasts, cold gelatined game, slices of venison; fish from the sea and the rivers filled the golden plates; rosy fruits, heavy bunches of grapes filled the baskets; flagons overflowed with wines, red as the gooseberry or golden as the wheat.

"Thus is compensated whoever believes and hopes," said Corentin.

"Praised be God who made such largess," cried Gradlon. "Praised be His servant Corentin, through whom is revealed to us His bounty."

The cook approached.

"Lord monk, how did you manage so much by only plunging your hand into a fountain? If so many goods come to us from the piece of the body of one little fish, what would we be able to bring forth by pulling a bow on a stag or a wild boar or some of the other beasts who pass near here?"

But Corentin admonished the cook, saying:

"The benefits of the Lord do not cause pain to his creatures."

And leading the cook to the side of the spring, he showed him the little fish lately cut in two, now frolicking and making ripples in the pool as if nothing had happened.

At this new miracle, the king was filled with admiration and respect. He said to Corentin: "What do you do in this solitude, you to whom God has chosen to manifest Himself? Assuredly He desires you to teach the unbelieving and to carry to us all the light of His commandments."

Corentin answered with humility:

"The ways of the Lord are full of mystery. All that has been produced, He ordained, that His will be accomplished."

"Venerable hermit," responded the king of Cornouaille, "you will leave your rough dress, your belt of hemp, your home of boughs. You will accompany me to Quimper. I shall name you bishop. You will wear a mantle of gold and a tunic of linen. You shall have my palace for your dwelling, and you shall govern the city by the law of God."

"Lord," said Corentin, "thus will I do, since it is through your mouth that God has chosen to instruct me. But, alas, what will become of my disciples scattered in the forest of Armorica who, under my rule, seek the ways of virtue? What will these sheep do if their pastor abandons them? How will the children live if the father is removed?"

"Reassure yourself, lord monk," said the king. "I know a place well open to the rising and the noontime sun, well sheltered from harsh winds, and for this it is called Landévenec. There I shall build the largest monastery in the world. It will have one hundred clocks, notched ramparts, lordly donjons. All your monks of today and tomorrow will live there. It will be a place of freedom and refuge. And you will be the abbot, holy man Corentin."

Then the hermit blessed God in His works, and, mounted on a mule, he guided the king's retinue back through the ways of the forest.

Dahut

IN QUIMPER SOON WERE BUILT richly gilded basilicas and churches, monasteries and cloisters, surrounded by deep moats and solid walls. Learned and pious monks flocked there. All day and night there mounted toward the heavens, with the sound of holy bells, concerts of hymns and fervent prayers.

Under the prudent rule of Corentin the common folk softened their manners, and the lords moderated their passions. Where there had been only debauchery, grossness, lying and impropriety, there now flowered decency, humility, charity, all the healthy virtues of the righteous.

The noble bishop took over his task firmly. He governed with gentleness and prudence, reprimanding vice and encouraging virtue, applying the canons and the laws of the synods.

And these were his ordinances: That violence and cruelty be forbidden. That clerics avoid the company of strange women; for although it is bad for man to be alone, familiarity with such women is dangerous to clerics because it invites them to sin; and that clerics violating this prohibition be defrocked. That virgins consecrated to God who voluntarily fall into sin be deprived of Communion, and be removed from the altar of the faithful. That those who marry women with husbands still living incur excommunication. That among married men only those having had one wife, married as a virgin, be admitted to higher orders. That public penance be allowed those who confess their faults and show repentance.

Thus by the virtue of the bishop, peace replaced discord, faith put away defiance, happiness and prosperity conquered worry and misery. King Gradlon in his palace enjoyed this tranquility and blessed God who had sent him this holy man Corentin. His contentment would have been perfect if

Dahut, his daughter, had given in as did all others to the tender ministry of the holy monk and bowed her young face in the sanctuaries.

Dahut had grown. The years had made her marvelously beautiful. She was tall, her body supple and well formed; her face had always a strange paleness amidst her tawny hair. Her eyes, which never lowered under another's gaze, ordinarily expressed boldness and command; in anger they burned with a terrible fire ready to consume all. In desire her eyes half closed, letting pass only a gentle caressing gleam. No one was able to resist the light or the demand of those eyes.

In measured words, however, the holy man Corentin carried his complaints to the king.

"Lord king, for the glory of Christ and yours, everyone in this place is open to my precepts except the one you love so much, your daughter, Dahut."

"What are you saying, holy bishop?" said Gradlon, showing his astonishment.

"Alas! Lord, how may the people persevere in their good ways if the example does not come from those who are in charge of giving it to them?"

"What?" said Gradlon. "Are you not entirely pleased with me? Have I not given you full control over this city? Am I not a good model for your flock?"

"It is not about you that I am concerned. It is your daughter, Dahut, whom I have named."

"And of what do you accuse her, good bishop?"

"She offends God through her fine clothes which hardly express a modest soul."

"Consider," said Gradlon, "she is so beautiful, and she takes great care to please me. Is this so grievous a sin?"

"Sire, she offends God by her frivolous words, she scoffs at the priests, turning their teachings into mockery."

"Think; she is no more than a child, at the beginning of her youth. Is that so grievous a sin?"

"She does not frequent the churches; she is rarely seen in the chapel on her knees listening to the gospel and confessing her guilt."

"Think; at her age songs are preferable to sermons, games to devotion. Is that so grievous a sin?"

"Oh, sire," said Corentin sadly, "a father's love is blind. Let us hope no chastisement comes to us from God because of this."

"Holy man," responded King Gradlon, "end this torment. To Dahut, my daughter, whom indeed I love so much, I shall speak as it is suitable.

Through love of me she will then quiet your fears and put herself under your rule."

"Then God be with you, lord king, in this paternal duty. Truly, it is a difficult task."

Gradlon summoned his dear daughter, Dahut with the green eyes and tawny hair, and very calmly—since he was able to feel neither rancor nor anger against her—chided her gently about that which the bishop had mentioned.

But Dahut did not submit as a mare under the whip; she quivered and reared, her pupils suddenly full of rage.

"Erstwhile," she cried, "one found in Quimper ease and liberty; all wore the clothes and jewels they wished in their own way, and everywhere I met laughing faces, holiday coiffures, colorful bands. Today there are only brown robes, close-shaven heads, and grey visages. Young people resemble old, gaiety no longer has refuge here, and your monks, lord, will soon lead us all about to the tune of a funeral litany."

"Here," said the king irritated, "I will not suffer even you to speak so of my religious men."

"Father," replied the child, "seek within the city for houses decorated with flowers, clothes of fine textiles, and lacework; seek money and gold. Your quest will be in vain. All goes to the monks. All goes to fill their coffers, to increase their secret treasuries. There disappear heritages, gifts and taxes taken from the people. At great expense to us, churches and cloisters are built each day, already more numerous now than the stars in the sky, more tightly packed than the grain of the field."

Gravely Gradlon said, "Before all, daughter, God must be served and glorified. From Him come all the goods of the earth, and if this is returned to Him, that is justice."

Then Dahut bent her head and cried. And the king of Cornouaille could not see without weakness or regret, the tears of his child.

"Daughter, ask and you shall have of me anything that you desire—except that which is God's, our Master's."

"Father," she said, "what can you do for me? Are you not a prisoner of these wicked monks? Though you are, I am not. Since they slander me to you and you listen to them, alas, there is nothing they have left you able to do for me."

Gradlon lifted his brows with pride.

"I am the king, Dahut, and I repeat to you: except that which is God's, you can have all that is here if you wish it."

Joy came again to the innocent face of Dahut. Her voice became soft;

charmingly she twined her caressing arms around the enchanted king.

"Good lord," she said, "I wish only one thing of this world: the sea."

"That is a mysterious wish, daughter."

"The sea," continued Dahut, "on which I was born; the sea, which received the beautiful body of Queen Malgven as you have told me many times. . . . Oh, father, remember how we mingled our tears while you told me of it."

"I remember, Dahut, and my heart bleeds yet."

"And mine, father, suffers as an exile. Away from the sea I languish, I suffocate, I die. Ah! I believe that the waves roll their foam in my veins, that in my hair the tempest blows. My raptures and my cries are the echo of the ocean, my beauty is but a reflection of its waves. I feel it beat, roar, and abate by turns. Away from the sea all is ennui and sadness."

Gradlon sighed. "How then can I satisfy you, my child? In another time I would willingly have put you on a fast ship. I would have sailed with you at the will of the winds toward unknown lands. But this is no longer the time for perilous navigation and harsh conquests. How can I soften your pain?"

He kissed her tenderly, and Dahut said to him:

"Lord, you can see to it. Build for me at the very edge of the sea a new city."

"A city!" cried the king. "In what place?"

"In a wild and desolate place, far from your forests full of hermits, far from your city full of monasteries."

"Dahut, Dahut, what do you wish there?"

"Thus, oh father, you will give me great pleasure and a long life. I know a deserted bay at a point where Cornouaille is no longer before me but only the infinite sea. Build me a city there, white and radiantly beautiful. There will be no other horizon than that where the sky rejoins the sea. The walls of the city will be bathed by the waves, over its roofs the seabirds will soar."

"Daughter, that is idle fancy and madness."

"As a child I have played on this shore, skipped the flat pebbles, collected the sea shells which well up in the murmur of the sea. There I wish to live, lord, if it is agreeable to you."

The good king smiled.

"This, beloved daughter, would entail great care and expense. I will think on it, but I hardly dare to promise."

Then in secret he called together his builders and gave orders and with them he made a plan of the new city.

"Sire," they said, "this enterprise is complete madness. There is not a road over which we could transport goods to this deserted shore."

"I shall lay out roads," responded the king, "and I will send as many workmen as are needed. The road will be finished faster than will be the wagons."

"That is well, lord, but it is not enough. The tides rise high at this place, and our barges will be unable to reach it."

"I will carve out a channel for transport barges. I will build walls which will shelter it from the sea."

"Then we will do your will, sire."

"Go and serve me promptly."

They set to work so intensely that soon both night and day that savage bay resounded with the sound of picks, of saws, of hammers. The ocean seemed astonished, and recoiled before the workers. From hour to hour the granite ramparts grew harder, the stonework towers grew taller, and the shadow of that marvelous city spread out upon the ocean.

Meanwhile Dahut questioned her father, sometimes humbly and beggingly, sometimes boldly and angrily.

"Lord, my father, will you not give me that which claims my heart: a city on the shore of the sea?"

"Patience," said the king. "I have not decided. One is wise who thinks a long time before making up his mind."

"Father, from your cruelty I shall die."

"Nay."

"Father, I shall die, I say to you, if you do not content me."

But always he offered her some reason: that the place was not ready for work, that the treasury was empty, that there was a lack of builders, that war was near, and a hundred other reasons for delay or refusal.

"Oh," she moaned, "all that you say may well be true, but perhaps this my fantasy is worth more than wisdom."

Thus early in the morning Dahut began her prayer, and thus he responded to her, laughing to himself, the good King Gradlon. While with money and with threats he pushed the construction, hardly allowing any rest because he wished nothing more on earth than a smile on the lips of Dahut, than happiness in the eyes of Dahut, his child so beloved.

One day finally the king said:

"Daughter, good counsel came to me while sleeping. That is, to go to this shore of which you speak, and if it is possible for an entire city to be built there by the hand of man, I swear to God it will be lifted up there for your pleasure."

He mounted his horse, Morvack. Dahut took her horse, the color of fire, and they rode together without stop as far as the furthest point of Cornouaille, to the place where from all sides one could see only the immensity of the water.

And suddenly from a high spot of the road Dahut saw at her feet the new city, all beautiful and white just as she had described it, surrounded by the foam of the waves, radiant under the sun.

Dahut clasped her hands over her breast and cried:

"Oh, father, this time I shall die, not of sadness, but of joy."

And Gradlon said to her:

"All this belongs to you, Dahut. Take the city, I give it to you."

Happily they urged their horses toward the ramparts. And thus was founded the city of Ys.

The Korrigans

OF ALL THE CITIES IN THE WORLD none surpassed Ys in splendor. The public squares were large, the avenues spacious, the houses beautifully aligned and of pleasant appearance with façades of smooth stone or enameled brick, with roofs of scarlet and trim of vivid colors.

In the port were boats; in the market place were fishermen, merchants, strollers all gaily clothed, all cheerful and noisy as happy people.

At this sight Dahut was not able to control herself. She laughed, she cried. She thanked the king at each instant, completely softened. She heaped presents and gold upon the builders, masons, carriers, painters, artisans, masters or valets. She was generous to the drivers of convoys, to the workers of the pulleys. Men and beasts ate and drank to their fill. The celebration lasted many days and it was marvelous to see the games, the feasting, the gallantries which took place there.

Gradlon soon found that his treasuries were empty, and he chided his treasurer, who in turn blamed all the follies:

"Sire, ordinarily you are prudent of your spending, even saving your small coins. But now you have exhausted your treasury by building and decorating the city of Ys."

"Good man," responded the king, "we shall summon the lenders."

"And what will you give them in pledge for a loan, your domains?"

"Very well."

"They are mortgaged, lord king, for their value. Your jewels?"

"Certainly."

"They are as well, and your precious tableware, and your crown."

"Then, good man, we shall go to war and make conquests to win what is needed. Tributes and pillages will fill our coffers. But do not speak to me of economies or I shall dismiss you. Because nothing matters to me now except to please Dahut, my daughter, to hear Dahut laugh and sing, and to put in her little hands all the gold of Cornouaille."

And he undertook other celebrations and commanded more sumptuous feasts and everyone in Ys took part, praising and acclaiming Gradlon. Thus time passed without bringing an end to these pleasures.

However, one day a servant came to tell the king:

"Lord, a messenger has come to you from Quimper, the envoy of Bishop Corentin."

This messenger was a severe monk, with serious eyes and the pallid cheek of one who is fasting.

Courteously the king welcomed and greeted him:

"Sir monk, God will that your news be good to hear. Gaiety is mistress here; to disturb it would be a mortal sin, for which it would be necessary for me to obtain remission for you from your holy pastor."

"King Gradlon," said the monk, "in Quimper the Bishop Corentin is sad. His soul grieves at reports carried to him from this city of Ys which is now your residence."

"Well," said the king, "what disturbs him about my city of Ys? Have I not made him judge of all on his land? What more does he want of me?

"For himself, nothing, lord king, but for God the glory and the homage due to Him."

"And how am I at fault, good monk?"

"Lord, Corentin knows human malice, and he suspects the truthfulness of reports. That is why he spoke to me in this way: 'Be my sight in Ys; see if, as I have been informed, there is there not one place, not an acre of soil, where God is adored.' And I entered into Ys, I have looked around me. I have explored the most remote quarters seeking a temple where I might kneel before the Most High. I have crossed the palaces, I have walked in the shadow of lofty towers, I have stopped before stalls full of merchandise. Nowhere have I discovered a house of God."

At these words Gradlon bent his head. The monk went on:

"Here then, oh king, is what Bishop Corentin orders: he who builds his house before having built the house of God is not worthy to be counted among the servants of Christ. If before Christmas Day a house of God is not erected in Ys, more superb than the most superb already built, more rich than the most rich, then the curse of the All Powerful will be on this city and on those who inhabit it, on the stone which shields it, and on the warriors who defend it, on the earth which carries it, and even on the sea which beats against its walls."

This speech made King Gradlon unhappy and he promised the messenger to do what the bishop had ordered. But when he was alone he fell into a great hesitation. He had not built churches because Dahut had not wished it and he dreaded the anger of Dahut no less than the threat of the bishop.

At the same time the people of Ys presented themselves to him saying:

"Lord king, we would have only praise for your city if it were not that by misfortune it is lower than the sea. When the sea rises the water overruns our wharves, and our homes. Each evening we are chased by the influx and forced to take refuge on the rocks. Our homes are flooded and spoiled, our furniture swept away, our produce lost."

"This is a hard trial for you, my friends."

"Lord, what will you do against this evil?"

"Alas, friends what should I do?"

"Raise for us a dike to keep out the ocean."

"Brave people, if I raise a dike against the ocean how will your boats leave port?"

They responded: "Between the dike and the city you will construct, sire, a deep basin closed by thick doors. When the tide rises, the doors will open and the water will lift up our boats; at high tide the basin will be closed; when the sea ebbs, it will be opened again and we will sail out with the water."

And the fishermen added that in emptying the basin they would gather enough fish and shellfish to nourish the entire city in times of storm and dearth.

But the king wavered, and Dahut in her turn pressed him.

"Father, listen to your people, answer their request, because if you do not, the fishermen and merchants will leave for a place where they will have better fortune. Ys will be like a desert, and we shall perish of boredom."

Then Gradlon cried out:

"Who are the people to complain of their unsafe houses when God Himself has no house at all?"

Dahut flushed with emotion, her green eyes caught fire with fury. She bit her lips:

"Lord, it seems to me the Bishop Corentin has given you a scolding."

Gradlon responded, "The Bishop Corentin is a just and holy man. The sign of God is on his forehead, the truth of God is in his mouth. Shame to me that I have sadly offended him. It is not a dike, it is not a basin that is necessary in Ys. It is a consecrated church, a pious sanctuary, that is required."

And heated from his resolution he called his architects and his builders, and commanded them to go to work immediately.

"In the time that it takes a swallow to build his nest you will construct in the best square a church which God claims as His right. Its roof will dominate all other roofs. Its wall will be decorated with gold. Its entrance steps will be of marble, the doors of wrought silver. And in the time that I have fixed, bells will sound from its tower and on its altar will burn the sacred flame. If this be not accomplished, you will be condemned and hung as false and evil servants."

The architects and the builders trembled. They looked at each other full of fears, and the king dismissed them without their daring to utter a word.

Then, in the time it takes a swallow to build its nest, they constructed for Gradlon a church with a double wall surrounding the holy place, and doors turned toward the east, so lofty that they attracted from afar the gaze of all, the ungodly as well as the faithful. A great square courtyard stood before the doors, bordered by a gallery of columns. In the middle of this courtyard were fountains of gold running with abundant fresh water. Three doors opened in the façade. The principal door was of wrought silver, the others of copper with inlays of silver. Through the great door one entered the nave, through the small doors, the sides, where there were windows covered by trellises of wood, all in a beautiful style and agreeably painted. The nave was carried on massive columns, the walls shone with precious metals and rich jewels, the floors were marble mosaics of intricate designs. Around the altar were thrones for the priests, the most magnificent destined for the bishop. A wooden screen, admirably decorated, enclosed the sanctuary. All was rich and well finished and worthy of God.

And on the day fixed by the king, the bells rang in the church, candles burned on the altar. All the city cried out at the miracle.

But at the sight Dahut fell into a swoon, and tears poured from her eyes. She stayed in her room, wild and angry. In vain her servants tried to console her; vainly her father beseeched her to be comforted, promising to accede to her slightest wishes. Nothing could draw her from her grieving.

But when night came she ran to the port, threw herself into her boat and went out on the open sea. The sea was as calm as a pond. The new moon mounted its thin crescent from the horizon. Alone, Dahut rowed hard, her heart full of excitement, her cheeks distended with her effort, her beautiful hair all undone floating in the lively air of evening.

The isle of Sein is feared by pilots. They say that none navigates there without shipwreck. There, in the shelter of a deep woods, living in seclusion, are the priestesses of the ancient cult of the Armoriane, the Senes. In olden times ships bearing many gifts sailed to them from the Veneti and from Nantes, from Brittany and even from some of the Latin countries, because the Senes had enchantments to excite or appease the tempests, to foretell

perilous adventures, to cure mortal sicknesses. But the God who came from the East had troubled their celebrations and dispersed their gatherings, and the virgins of the isle were forsaken on their wild rock with only the seabirds as companions.

Dahut rowed to the island and as soon as she touched land she darted down the stone paths to the retreats of the Senes. She searched long in the uninhabited woods and on the deserted beaches. Finally she perceived the priestesses, seated in the middle of a clearing where the moon threw a weak light.

Entering the circle of light, she cried in a strong voice:

"Oh Senes, listen to me! This is Dahut, princess of Cornouaille, come to seek your aid."

The eldest of the Senes responded:

"We know you well, Dahut, daughter of Gradlon. We have met you in the moors where they still celebrate in secret the mysteries of our gods. Rare are those who come to the tables of stone because the servants of the new God follow us to the depths of the forest, and lie in wait through the nights of the moon for the last adorers of Teutates."

Dahut replied: "It is true, my sister, that this God has filled our cities with churches and our countryside with monasteries. Alas, King Gradlon has abandoned Quimper to Him, and I have had to flee before Him. I had chosen for my refuge a city built with a good wall where no chapel wounded my sight, where the melancholy chanting of the monks no longer dominated the sweet melodies of the ocean. But now, by some awesome artifice, at the center of this city a church has risen up in less time than is necessary for a bird to make his nest. The Crucified One has constructed the dome, cast the bells, lighted the candles under the arch. I am conquered. I am humiliated. Where am I to go? What am I to do?"

The Senes asked: "What do you wish of us, Dahut?"

"In my soul," said Dahut, "I have begged Teutates, master of the world. Without success I have repeated the magic formulas which force the will of the immortals. And despairing, I address myself to you who possess sovereign charms and whose voice is always heard in the councils of the gods."

The Senes said: "The hour is favorable to invocation. See, the crescent of the moon appears above the trees, the wind blows from the north, the night bird has cast its plaintive cry three times. Speak. What is it you wish?"

Dahut responded: "In order to give a church to the Crucified One in my city of Ys, Gradlon, my father, has refused to build a dike which the people claim they need. I wish the dike to be built in one night."

"Is that, Dahut, all you desire?"

"In order to give a church to the Crucified One in my city of Ys, Gradlon, my father, has refused to hollow out the basin which the people petition. I wish the basin to be constructed in one night."

"Is that, Dahut, all you desire, in truth?"

"My desire is more ambitious, O my sister. The church of the Crucified One dominates the dwellings of Ys as the birch dominates the thicket. I wish tomorrow at dawn to have my castle rise up on the rocks of Ys, so high in the sky that its roofs tower over the church as the oak towers over the birch."

Then the Senes stood up and held up their arms toward the sky and the moonlight, and spoke thus to Dahut:

"Repeat after us the words we say: I call you, spirits of the air and of the earth, winged slaves of the gods, and you, subterranean spirits. I beg you, industrious Korrigans, quick elves. Hasten, obey my orders: during this night, may your skillful hands build the impassable dike, hollow out the basin, and set on the rocks of Ys the beautiful castle of Dahut."

When they finished the princess pronounced the same words. Then the Senes made a great fire of dry herbs. They kept it going in silence as long as the moon was visible in the sky. A thin veil of smoke covered the entire island, a black whirlpool churned by the wind slid over the surface of the waves.

When the fire was only ash the Senes said to Dahut:

"Return to your boat and do not touch the oars. The breath of the spirits will push you toward Ys and when you reach port you will see the work of the Korrigans."

"My sisters, here are my ornaments, my necklaces; here are the bracelets from my arms, they are yours. And I shall send you as much gold as can be carried in a barge manned by six oarsmen."

But they answered her: "Necklaces and bracelets are the joy of wives. What would the virgins of the isle do with jewelry? What can the Senes make with the gold you give them? They will die one after the other and with the last will die the old gods of Armorica."

In her boat, without touching the oars, Dahut travelled toward Ys. When she came near the port she saw on the rock a castle, the towers of which dominated the church of the Crucified One as the hundred-year-old oak dominates a thin birch. She saw a dike so high that no tide would be able to reach its top. She saw a spacious basin closed by bronze doors. And she gave a triumphant smile of content.

In the bronze doors hung some keys of silver, so fine, so prettily carved, so well polished that no human artisan could have made them, and Dahut as a sign of victory hung the silver keys at her neck by a chain of gold.

The Song of Dahut

WHEN THE PEOPLE OF YS WOKE and saw the dike and the basin and the thick bronze doors and the castle set on the hill, they uttered great acclamations and they assembled around the palace where the king slept. Gradlon heard their clamor, and asked its cause. His squires said to him:

"Lord king, during the night the dike and the basin of the port were made, and on the mountain a magnificent castle has been built. It must have been sorcery."

But Gradlon did not want to believe them. He went to the window and saw the marvels with his own eyes. He recognized among the people Dahut, his daughter, wearing the silver keys around her neck.

And he cried out completely terrified:

"How has this come about? Is it not the work of a demon?"

Dahut replied to him laughing:

"Lord, do not seek to know how this happened. You were able in only a few weeks to pull from the sand an entire city. You were able in only three days to construct a basilica. Why should I not have done in one night more than your builders did in three days?"

Gradlon drew her to him.

"Daughter, what are these keys at your neck, fastened by a chain of gold?"

"Father, these are the keys of the doors which enclose the city from the sea. These doors are of bronze, a foot thick. Twenty strong men are unable to move them."

She gave the silver keys to the king.

"Sire, take these keys as a mark of your power. No one here has the right to the city except through you."

But Gradlon, very troubled and overcome with worry, hesitated. Then Dahut kissed his hands, saying:

"For love of me, father, be guardian of these keys. Do not leave them day or night. Do not permit them to be out of your possession, save when they are used to open and close the gates of bronze, and that only in your presence."

The king obeyed his beloved daughter and hung around his neck the silver keys on the golden chain.

"I shall not leave them," he said, "upon my life."

Meanwhile the people of Ys were blessing Dahut and saying:

"Through her we are assured goods and profits of all sorts. She has only to wish it, and our granaries and storehouses will be filled without our effort."

They said this over and over in many words and finally dispatched some men to the princess.

"Lady, evil is the sea on the coast where it pleased you to have your city. In terrible storms, many set out who do not return. Alas, in more than one house there are already tears and lamentations. Will you do nothing for your friends?

Dahut answered them:

"I shall build some ships which will master the sea even through terrible storms, so your affairs will prosper and in your houses no one will cry anymore."

She took herself to the moors in a place called Teil where the high stone tables were set up. There she invoked the Korrigans, as the Senes had taught her. The day after, the people found in the port of Ys a hundred ships bridged and masted, with long keels and new sails.

However, some time later the people of Ys came to Dahut, groaning once more.

"Who says fish says poverty. What fortune it would be, beautiful lady, to go beyond the seas to buy valuable produce for the markets of Cornouaille and of France. And willingly would we do this if we had some ships fitted to sail far distances."

And Dahut listened to them. The Korrigans at her voice moored in the port good vessels curved at the prow and at the stern, ready to sail to distant shores and through any storms.

The people of Ys were happy for only a moment.

"Why," they complained, "should we navigate at great peril on the changing sea? Why depend for our riches on the hazards of the waves? Each day rival ships sail by, carrying all that we must sail so far to obtain. But these ships are more rapid than ours, we cannot overtake them, and they are sailed

by bold warriors so that we could not attack them without misfortune. Only Dahut, our princess, would be able to take them if it pleases her."

At their supplication Dahut graciously responded.

"Ah, will you never be content with me? But I love you and wish my city of Ys to flourish more than all other cities. So I will do your will and, if you will have it so, no vessel shall pass peaceably by your shores."

And by night she descended toward the ocean, barefoot on the sand. And through magic formulas she called forth from the unfathomable depth of the sea, and from the deep grottoes of the rocks, a thousand dragons of terrible visage and of tremendous force. Their bodies were covered with scales harder than bronze; their tails beat the sea, lifting up a spray of foam. Their backs were covered with enormous spines and their throats spewed forth burning darts. At Dahut's call, they sped toward the beach like savage horsemen galloping over the plains. From their mouths came raucous sounds like water beating against the cliffs.

To each inhabitant of Ys the daughter of Gradlon gave one of these monsters; and the monsters, more docile and patient than oxen, dashed into the sea at the will of their masters and hunted the rival ships laden with wheat, oil, and spices, the galleons which transported rare metals, amber, and sandalwood to the north.

The people of Ys became so rich that they drank their wine and barley beer only from goblets of gold, and measured their grain only with silver baskets. From all countries people came to their markets, their ships sailed all the rivers. It was said that the poorest of the city of Ys was yet richer than a king.

At the palace of Dahut the magician, the Korrigans had accumulated wonderful things. The walls were covered with gold, mother-of-pearl and coral. The beds were purple and rose, the walls were hung with canopies of silk. The ceilings, the doors, and the walls surrounding the gardens were of brilliant metal. The stables had marble floors with tiles varied according to the color of the horses—white as snow, red as fire, black as storm clouds.

The Korrigans, swift and invisible, took perfect care of the castle, diverting a river's course so that it crossed and washed the stables and the palace. They took the same care of the city of Ys. They fed the sea-dragons penned up in the basin and at the hour of the changing tide it was they who opened and closed the great bronze gates, a task beyond the strength of the most vigorous of men.

But these doors could be opened only at the order of Gradlon. Each time he detached the silver keys from the gold chain around his neck, and each time he replaced them, for he had confidence in none else to keep them. Even in his sleep he wore the silver keys on the gold chain.

At evening when everyone had closed his dwelling, one might see a form draped in white descending to the beach by steps cut in the rock. It was Dahut. Weary from the pleasures of the day, trembling in the fresh breeze, she would glide over the sands, drop her white veils, and abandon her beautiful body to the ocean. For a long time she lay in the waves which supported her and rocked her as the hands of a lover. She would plunge and reappear, the waves lifting her up, the water dripping from arms bathed in a rosy light. Her pale flesh seemed to melt in the foam, as she stretched herself on a dark wave, like a mother-of-pearl shell which the water gently carried to the shore.

And then on the beach she stood naked, and while she combed her long hair flecked with gold, she sang. And this is what she sang:

I was born on yonder sea, far away, amid the fog.
The Ocean wind carried my first cries.
The breath of the storm scattered my first sounds.

I was born on the sea.
The water was grey as ash,
the sky was covered by clouds.
The sails flapped in shreds,
the ropes hissed in the air like angry snakes.

I was born on the sea.
In vain the desperate pilot pressed the rudder;
the oarsmen breathlessly struggled in vain
against the waves, and their cries with each attempt
mingled with the cries of my mother torn.

I was born.
And suddenly the sky opened, azure adorned,
the water became blue,
the sun pierced the mist as the arrow
pierces the hart in flight.
And my mother took me in her weakened hands
and my father stooped over me to see my smile;
and the sailors extended toward me
their blood-stained hands.

The ship rocked gently to and fro
as a willow cradle.
The wave was my attentive nurse;
the light foam kissed my little fingers.

I breathed lungfuls of salty air.
I cried with joy when bands of alegons
with their wide wings passed by.
As a game my father waved in front of
my eyes his lance decorated with horsehair.

One day my mother pressed me to her
so tightly that I cried.
And when they took me from her arms,
there were tears in all their eyes.

The waves opened to receive
the beautiful queen.
She had a helmet on her head,
her body was clothed in a blue hauberk;
a shield hid her legs;
a lance lay across the shield.

All that is what my father told me
when I was of an age to understand;
and he said to me the queen
resembled a sleeping Valkyrie
as in the Songs of the North.

On the beach, combing dry her wild hair, Dahut recited also this other
poem:

Beautiful Ocean who saw me born,
you rocked me as a mother.
And when I was a child
you played with me as an elder sister.

Now I am grown and beautiful,
my hair covers my back,
my breasts are white and full.
Take me in your arms as a lover.

Take me in your arms;
they are so strong they overturn
the highest rocks,
so gentle that they touch
the sand lightly without
disturbing a grain.

But for me your arms
will always be gentle and caressing.
You will not shatter me on a reef;
you will not carry me down to your black abyss.

I call you and you come, docile as the war horse
that I love. I call you and you kneel at my feet,
and you take me away on your silver back,
you bound on liquid plains.

Anon, jealous lover, you roll me in your cloak
to hide my nakedness from the skies;
anon, proud lover, you carry me as a superb flower,
as the most beautiful jewel in your coffers.

What will you give me as a present of love?
What will you give me as a gift of espousal?
What ornament will you seek from your innumerable treasures?
You are not an everyday lover.
I am hardly a common fiancée.
I want neither the white veils,
nor the crowns, nor the jewels of the others.

Oh, my lover! Oh, my slave!
What will you do to make me the most beautiful
and the most desired of women,
that in front of me all eyes will light up,
and all lips go pale?

You will draw from your shadowed depths
the pearls whose light resembles
that of the twilight.
You will offer them to me in purple shells,
and let them envy the mother-of-pearl
of my neck and shoulders,
they will be effaced by the light of my skin.

You will bring from your chasms corals
as large as the trees and crowned with seaweed
as the forest is with leaves.
They are less red than my mouth,
less rosy than my polished nails.

And the fish of your depths—
the fish with colors of the opal
variable as your waters—
you will strew them on my path;
my eyes are more brilliant than their scales,
more capricious than the light on the waves.

You will give me the riches of the wrecked ships
in your depths, all the treasures which you have
guarded as a miser, never to reappear.
Why have you broken on these reefs
so many ships full of riches?
Why have you killed so many sailors?
For whom are you sowing with wreckage the deserted beaches?
I will have all the goods that forgotten galleons carried.
I will have all which cost so many lives,
so many tears of wives and mothers.
But my desire is as immense as you,
beautiful Ocean, my love.
The treasures which you will give me will please me
but an instant.

I wish the heart of all the men who catch my eye,
of all those whose name will brush my lips,
of all those whom my caprice discerns.

I wish husband to leave wife for me,
that brother hate his brother,
that father drive away his children.
I wish no one I have chosen ever to refuse me.

All these lovers you will give to me,
Oh, my jealous lover! Oh, my lord!
Oh, my beautiful, furious Ocean!
And I shall serve you in your turn—
for all these lovers shall I deliver to your fury!

I will deliver them to you under the spell of my caress,
lulled to sleep by my embraces,
and you will take from them your vengeance.
You will smother them in your grasp,
you will lay their remains on the tips of your reefs.

And you will avenge me thus in my timeless weakness,
because I am not able to master my heart,
to extinguish the fire which burns in my senses.

But for me you will be always obedient, docile, tender.
Never will your anger turn against me,
never will your great voice resound to curse me.
For you love me and belong to me,
beautiful Ocean who saw me born,
you who rocked me as a mother,
you who played with me as a sister
when I was only a child.

Some fishermen reported that one evening the princess Dahut, coming up from the beach at the summit of the rock, had thrown her golden ring into the sea. An enormous wave, a whirlpool of foam, had shot forth, mounted the cliff and grasped as in an embrace the daughter of Gradlon.

At this marvel, the fishermen fled, not without hearing the piercing laugh of Dahut.

The Magic Mask

Day and night there was festivity at the castle built by the Korrigans above the rich city of Ys.

It was not in the home of Gradlon that these merrymakings took place. King Gradlon lived in a separate apartment, forsaken, almost alone. So great was his tenderness for Dahut, his beloved daughter, that he had given up restraining her or advising her. From one weakness to another he gave up all power, falling into idleness and melancholy.

But, in the quarters of Dahut, the festivals, games, and dances never ceased. From the city one saw until morning the windows lit by a thousand lights, one heard the songs and the laughing and the sounds of harps, the joyous hum of the guests.

And each time that she assembled her faithful, Dahut made a new lover sit next to her and she pressed herself to his side, put around his neck her beautiful white arms, enveloping him in her perfumed hair and kissing him on the lips in front of everyone. Then she commanded that he drink from the same cup as she, that he chew the piece of fruit which she marked with her teeth. Then she would grasp him around the neck and hold him prisoner until her blazing look made him quiver from desire, until she drew from him a painful cry. And everyone around the table applauded, and drank to Dahut's loves from their goblets of gold. And each man in himself burned to be he whom Dahut made quiver and cry under her glance.

For her came running from all the countries of the world the most illustrious sons. There came famous knights, great swashbuckling heroes and destroyers of citadels. They wore hauberks of double mail and bronze helmets, and some had wounds of glory. There came princes in golden litters, accompanied by squires, pages, falconers. They had horses with

coverings of purple and silver and they drank from goblets encrusted with precious stones. There came kings with large corteges, bringing with them their counselors, their bishops, their best vassals, and their favorites on carriages drawn by white horses with golden harnesses. There came wandering knights on fierce war horses; the knights were proud, ragged and quarrelsome. There came people with white hair, others hardly out of childhood. There came some who were beautiful and some who were ugly, some bold and some timid, some squanderers and some misers. There came some leading chariots full of goods and others who had sold their goods in order to equip themselves. There came some so sick and wasted that they gave up their souls at the threshold of the city.

And all, making their way by land or water, alone or accompanied, were drawn toward Ys because of Dahut, daughter of Gradlon of Cornouaille. And Gradlon received them with great affection. Dahut presented to them a gracious countenance, smiling on those who were young and well shaped. And all as soon as they looked upon the princess fell in love with her, losing their sense and their repose, no longer able to dream of returning to their homeland, but only to live and suffer near her.

Then in order to attract their lady, in order to please her and to be loved by her, they attempted prowess upon prowess, in the hunt, in tournaments, in witty games and clever words. Jealously they disputed among themselves for her look, her gesture, and they killed one another at the least word. Others, completely scorned, languished and died from a sickness without remedy.

Ah, so many hearts were smitten by Dahut, the beautiful. At Ys and in the region were many young men with lively eyes, tall build, deep laughter. There were sons of merchants, of fishermen, or serfs. In the crowds at the harbor when the adventuring ships departed, in the assemblies when the bards sang their lays, in religious festivals, in the moonlight on the moor, Dahut appeared, arousing in all of them burning desire. Each man that saw her, be it only for one time, was never able to forget her. She herself never forgot those whose beauty and strength had struck her. She inquired their names and their living place and guarded it well in her memory until the hour when her caprice was born.

Amid all who loved her was Sylven, page of Gradlon. Dahut had met him holding the torch at the door of the king. He had fine blond hair, a sweet grave face, his body was a little frail, his hands were very white; in his pale eyes shone his soul, loyal and candid. Before him Dahut had stopped suddenly, laughing and completely charmed.

From that day the youth had known neither peace nor sleep; in all moments, in all places he sought the princess, but if she approached he fled like a surprised robber or he became pale and trembling, his blood leaving his limbs so that he had to lean on the wall to keep from falling. Dahut, however, seemed indifferent, looking at him no more than at the stones of the path. But she saw him well, she felt the trouble and the fears of the gentle page; and maliciously she rejoiced in her heart, because she wished people to suffer and to cry for her.

Thus in great sorrow Sylven languished, neither sleeping nor taking nourishment, running like a fool through the city and the gardens, repeating senseless words, avoiding his friends and companions in games. He had a defeated look; his eyes were swollen from tears and lack of sleep.

And many teased him in passing:

"What is the cause of your sickness, Sylven? If it is your head, there are some good herbs and ointments; if it is your heart, there are beautiful girls to heal it."

But he fled from the teasing ones, saying to himself:

"There is neither herb nor ointment, there is not a mistress to cure me. Ah, surely I will die if God does not save me."

In the end he could stand it no longer and he thought to kill himself in order to escape his torment.

"What shall I do?" he sighed. "I am no longer able to live this way. I may well do something unreasonable for which I shall be ashamed and ridiculed. It is better to die."

In this mood, he had already sharpened his dagger to pierce his heart, when a man completely hidden in a black cloak came to his house. And this man said to him:

"Sylven, someone sent me who wishes you health and pleasure and who desires to see you promptly but in secret. Therefore, this evening, at dusk, go up to the castle on the rock, by the path which begins at the beach; at the end of the path is a low door, half veiled by brambles. Near them rises a tree, the branches of which touch the ground. Under this tree hide yourself and watch the door. When this door is opened, boldly show yourself."

Palpitating, and more pale than if the dagger had been in his flesh, Sylven asked:

"At this door, who awaits me?"

The man in the black cloak responded,

"Love and valor care little to know."

At this, Sylven understood that he had an audience with his lady, and he was overcome with joy. But the messenger said yet to him:

"Gentle page, take this silk mask, and when you come, place it over your face, so no one will recognize you. Your lady wishes it thus. If you do not do so, the low door of the castle will remain closed."

"I shall do it," cried Sylven.

And at dusk he ran to the indicated place, his face hidden by the mask. In an amorous fever he quivered and raved. The door was opened. He was drawn into a dark hall and led through subterranean passages and up stairways hewn in the walls, to the chamber where Dahut was lying on a bed of purple.

He threw himself at the feet of his mistress. Intending to pronounce a thousand sweet sentiments of love, he was able only to murmur, "Oh, my lady, here at this very instant I wish to die."

He believed it, and Dahut, bending over, kissed him on the lips slowly, as if to drink from them the life of the child. And when she had so kissed him she lifted him up and said to him:

"It is unseemly to die at the threshold of happiness; learn that, Sylven, and learn also that you will die only when I ordain it."

"Ah," he said, "when you ordain it, willingly shall I die."

He did not see the dark look of Dahut; perhaps he would have drawn back. But no, blind and vain are happy lovers, confidence is their law.

At dawn Dahut said to Sylven: "Lovely friend, here is the day and you must leave."

"Alas," he sighed.

Tenderly she replied, "Why moan after so charming a night?"

And Sylven, taking her in his arms, said,

"Ah! I curse the day which tears me away from you. How can I not hate it? How, sent away, shall I believe in my happiness? How shall I know I have not dreamed this dream, a humble page privileged to embrace the daughter of his king?"

Dahut smiled at him.

"It has nothing to do either with being page or king, Sylven; you are more noble of heart than the most noble, and the greatest of all if I love you."

And Sylven said:

"I shall enclose myself, pulling the curtains of my room in order not to be wounded by the sun. Thus I shall keep myself entirely in the shadow, to remember you until the evening which will bring me back to you."

"Yes, the evening. But leave now, friend, the hour is advanced."

When Sylven was departing, she called him back.

"Friend, do you love me?"

"You grieve me, most beloved. But test me, if doubts have come to you."

"Have you not already vowed that your life belongs to me?"

"Completely, Dahut."

"And if it please me to use my right?"

"I would bless you to do it."

"Child," she said, "go and be faithful to me. To return, follow the same way and the same guide who led you here. And please, do not fail to put the silk mask over your face so that no one will be able to recognize you because this would bring me great shame and injury through anger of the king."

She herself tied the ribbons which held the mask and gently pushed her friend away, closing her door.

Then Sylven, when he was outside, perceived the man in black who walked before him showing him the way. And as he arrived at the subterranean corridor, suddenly he felt the mask he wore grip him at the throat and temple, smothering him. He clutched at it to undo it but the mask was enchanted. The silk was changed suddenly into steel, and it strangled Sylven.

The child gave one cry, dropped to his knees, fell still and died.

The man in the black cloak, when he saw him outstretched, approached him, took from him the mask, and threw him over his shoulder. He approached the low door which led to the path. There waited a horse all black like his master. The man mounted to the saddle, having thrown the body of the page in front of him, and rode along the sea.

Near the Cape of Raz is the Gulf of Plogoff where the whirling water throws itself down with a terrible noise into the caverns of the deep. Around about, people say that it is one of the entrances to Hell. At the edge of the abyss of Plogoff, the man in black stopped his horse and let fall from the height of the cliff the body of the unfortunate Sylven.

Not far from this place some fishermen were pulling in their nets heavy with fish; but when they saw the man in the black cloak on the cliff, they abandoned their catch and fled, rowing full force without turning their heads.

Because many times people had met the mysterious horseman galloping at daybreak, carrying a burden across his saddle, the good people had affirmed that whoever dared to look him in the face suffered a horrible death.

Thus, the man in black went freely to deliver to the Ocean the lovers of the beautiful Dahut. Following a night of love, Dahut's caprice never lived beyond the first rays of morning.

Guenolé

ON THE ADVICE OF BISHOP CORENTIN, Gradlon had given the monastery of Landévenec to Guenolé, son of Fragan. This was a man of great wealth and property remarkable for his modesty and piety. A perfect discipline and a wise rule rendered his house famous and prosperous before all others.

Guenolé observed an austerity so severe that people everywhere looked at it as a gift of God that he was able to endure it without ruining his body. At all times he was clothed only in the skins of ox under which he wore a coarse hair shirt. He ate a bread mixed with ash, and this only twice a week. In the times consecrated to penance he slept on a bed of bark with a stone for a pillow. Never did he sit down, and he said the holy offices on his knees with his arms extended. In this state he was met with a measure of grace, ecstasy and divine visions, and was gifted with the ability to make miracles.

One day when Guenolé was at church praying in his customary posture and with great fervor, God showed Himself to him, appearing as one aggrieved. He spoke to him thus:

"Guenolé, if there are in this country many of my creatures who love me and serve me for their salvation, how many others act only to be lost, as do those in the city of Ys, whom you know on account of their vice and their debauchery."

"Alas, Lord," responded the holy man, "You know that not a day goes by when I do not pray and do mortification for that unhappy lost city, so that she will repent and leave her impiety."

"Ah, Guenolé, ten years of your prayers, ten years of your fasting would not atone for half of the sins committed there."

"What! Lord, to this point have they worn your patience?"

"They have so exhausted it that my wrath is upon them."

"Lord, my God, have pity because they are more blind than guilty. Do not strike them without giving them respite to free themselves from evil."

God said to Guenolé:

"Do you know well all the abominations which are done by the people of Ys?"

"Lord, they are rascals, lewd, adulterers. They blaspheme Your name and they love only the riches of this world. They follow not the divine offices; they do not enter Your temple. The church which was open to them is forsaken, so much so that weeds obstruct the threshold, nettles grow the length of the walls, and the swallow makes his nest under the portal."

"Is that all, Guenolé?"

"No, Lord; they frequent only the taverns and evil places; they drink wine and beer to excess; they care only to live for their own comfort and to abuse all their senses."

"Guenolé, are those all their sins?"

"No, Lord; they are vain of their bodies; they clothe themselves only in beautiful cloth of silk, of gold and of silver threads. They wear necklaces, jewelry, rings and bracelets. They cover themselves with perfume and makeup."

"Is there aught else, Guenolé?"

"Is this not enough to draw down your justice, O my God?"

"Ah! Guenolé, Guenolé, I would pardon them being greedy, impious, vain and debauched. I could pardon their laziness and faithlessness, but they have hearts more hard than the stone of the mountain. They no longer know how to survive without opulence. They chase away the poor as if they were ferocious beasts; they throw them into disgraceful jails or hang them. Never in one place have there been so many prisons. To all this Dahut, the daughter of Gradlon, enjoins horrible outrages to the body of the Savior. Know, my good servant Guenolé, that each day at her request, twenty of her knights take themselves, for love of her, to Communion in neighborhood chapels and they bring back to her the hosts which she throws to the pigs, or which she defiles in her orgies. Shall I suffer any longer such injury?"

Guenolé prostrated himself, his forehead on the ground.

"Lord, Your will be done!"

But God said to him again:

"The hour of justice is at hand. Here is what I command you, Guenolé: you will get up, you will go to this infamous city and warn them in my name that terrible will be their punishment if they do not repent on the instant."

Then Guenolé got up, tightened his cord belt and, taking a staff, left his beautiful monastery. He set out in haste. And walking along he thought:

"Infinite is the mercy of the Most High; one good action effaces the

worst crimes. Shall I not be able to find in this city a single element of salvation? Ah, with all my heart I shall exhort these sinners to penitence. I shall lead them back to good, if God will assist me."

He went, asking his bread from the villagers and the tenant farmers. Sleeping but little on the hard banks of the roads, he felt no fatigue.

And when he was at Ys, he saw the streets deserted, the houses empty. He passed before the church. Ah! As he had expected, there his soul was completely saddened: weeds and brambles covered the steps and the entrance; through the windows moved playful flocks of birds; the walls were worn away by wind and storm.

Guenolé, the holy man, sighed, and crossing the city, he arrived at the harbor where he met a great crowd of people. This was the hour when the doors of the dike were opened to let the rising sea enter and fill the basin. This maneuver, as Guenolé knew, was accomplished by the Korrigans whose presence there remained invisible. The crowd believed that these heavy doors moved by themselves through some secret energy, and they never failed to assemble at this spectacle.

The abbot of Landévenec, in his poor raiment, was not able to pass unnoticed among the people of Cornouaille, amply and richly dressed and coiffured with high headdresses. Soon he was surrounded by hostile clamor. Then one said:

"What is this beggar, this eyesore, this bringer of bad luck, this bird of ill omen?"

Another made way for him holding his nostrils. Another harshly cried out:

"To the noose with the leper! Do we not have any more rope for the unwelcome of this sort?"

And without a doubt the recluse would have been vilely treated, had there not arisen near by a terrified cry. The crowd suddenly wavered and moved off, retreating toward the city.

It happened that as the basin was filled, the bronze doors, instead of closing as usual, stood gaping. This was done through the will of God, or rather, because the Korrigans, aware of the presence of the holy monk Guenolé, had fled, as demons, gnomes and ghosts always do before the chosen of the Lord. So the water continued to overflow the dike, rising in the harbor, and threatening the city.

Twenty men darted forth, but the swelling waves, already dashing over the jetty, threw them back as pieces of straw and rolled their bodies on the beach.

Then Guenolé, seeing the peril, broke through the panic-stricken crowd, invoking the name of God. He advanced toward the boiling sea, and placing his feet on the water he continued to walk as easily as on the street of the harbor, as on the dry earth of a beautiful road; and when he reached the height of the bronze doors he touched them saying:

"Through the virtue of Christ, close yourselves."

And the doors closed immediately. Guenolé returned, gliding lightly over the waves, and the crowd which awaited him mute from stupor gave way before him. Then when he was in the middle of them he cried out:

"Friends, learn the ways of God! He has led me to you who have so sorely offended Him, and at once He gives you a proof of His mercy and preserves you from a great disaster. This is why you must search within your souls, deplore your faults and repent, and God will receive you in His goodness."

And he added:

"You have built against the sea and you have used him in wicked enterprises; but the sea is stronger than you; he will overrun you and will submerge your homes. Likewise you have built against God in your souls, but God will break you if you do not appease Him promptly."

And he urged them to do penance and to seek their salvation in renouncing earthly things for love of things eternal. Around him men and women bowed their heads and when he had finished, they went away grave and silent. Some of them approached Guenolé and, kissing his feet, spoke thus to him:

"Holy man, keep us under your safeguard and teach us, as we wish to confess and expiate our sins."

Guenolé was joyous and he blessed them.

"Go," he said, "and keep faith."

The next day he descended again into the city to fulfill his mission. But he soon perceived that the miracle of the night before had been forgotten; at his passage the citizens laughed and overwhelmed him with gibes; the children followed him dancing and throwing stones at him, and Guenolé heard the people speak thus of him:

"There is the wicked sorcerer, the maker of magic. If we do not beware, misfortune will overcome us."

When night came, God appeared to Guenolé:

"My good servant, persist no longer; these people have eyes and do not wish to see, they have ears and do not wish to hear. The punishment is ready."

But Guenolé begged Him:

"Lord, my God, hold back yet Your wrath. Allow me to attempt once more to convince them. I have not lost hope."

And, full of faith, he went again to the city, prevailing on some, chastising others. The season was warm; the sun burned cruelly on the sand, on the walls and in the open squares; but Guenolé did not feel the burning of the air, so carried away was he by his zeal. But he was astonished to find on his way only alarmed people and whispering groups. He noticed that the water was beginning to fail and the springs were drying up from the extreme heat. Already, to save water, they had slaughtered the useless animals.

The fourth day, the water failed completely. This provoked a gathering of the population and lively complaints, which reached the chateau of Gradlon, severely disturbing the king and his daughter.

In this danger Dahut in vain invoked the Korrigans, formerly docile to her orders. They no longer responded, frightened away by the virtue of the holy man of Landévenec.

When Guenolé appeared in the public place among the assemblage, a thousand suspicious looks stopped him and one of the malcontents designated him:

"That one is the cause of our evils. Since the coming of this monk, the ocean has wished to overwhelm us; and now the wells are dry, the fountains no longer flow, and we must die of thirst. We should have closed the city to the accursed one or chased him away. But now it is too late. May he be punished for his evil-doings."

"Friends," responded Guenolé, "your evil is born of yourselves, and not of others; and these evils are nothing compared to those which are foretold if you do not enter resolutely into penitence."

These words, far from calming the people, irritated them against the holy man. Already the more violent of them surrounded Guenolé, impatient to maltreat him. But he, turning on them his calm and gentle look, asked of them:

"What is the subject of your complaint?"

"Rascal," they said, "you know it well. The water fails in the wells and the fountains. Where shall we find it?"

Guenolé replied:

"From the spring from which springs the only water fresh and healthful as much for the body as for the soul."

And climbing up again to the city they walked toward the hill on which was constructed the marvelous chateau of Dahut, and the crowd followed him without ceasing to grow larger and full of complaints. At the base of the rock he turned toward his companions.

"Will you," he asked "confess the living God, if He, receiving you in His pity, makes surge from this dry rock a clear spring?"

They all cried in one voice:

"We shall confess Him."

Then Guenolé struck the rock with his staff. Under the blow sprang forth a spring so abundant that it formed a large stream which coursed toward the sea.

And the people fell to their knees, crying and loudly praising God. And Guenolé said to them:

"As from the rock springs forth this precious stream which will never run dry, so may your faith be sincere and lasting; by that all your sins will be redeemed; by that will be made your salvation."

Forthwith he opened the church, where he admitted numerous faithful to penance. And many of them forswore their goods in favor of the poor.

Alas, three days had not yet passed, when the church again became deserted. To their pleasures, to their loves, had returned the people of Ys. And God appeared again to the holy man in a dream:

"Guenolé, Guenolé, your zeal is without profit, my judgment is pronounced: you will not render life to those who are of decay, you will not give to the worms of the earth wings to lift them to the sky."

And Guenolé begged Him without ceasing:

"Lord, if my works are agreeable to You, do not take from me this trial; suspend your decree. Let these unhappy people have a last chance of pardon."

God answered him:

"Oh, my good servant, your works are such a joy to Me that I shall grant you this favor. But if they resist you still, no new entreaty will move Me."

A short time later there took place in Ys beautiful ceremonies and rejoicings for the anniversary of the birth of Dahut, beloved daughter of the king. And this was the occasion of so many orgies, such vile and shameful actions, that the good Guenolé lamented, wondering if he should not renounce his mad task.

During this festival there was there a great tournament and the monk was drawn along by the curious to the field where the tournament was being held. On the dais under a scarlet canopy, King Gradlon had taken his place, smiling at Dahut, seated at his side. His eyes never left her for an instant so fondly he loved her. Ah, without this love beyond measure, how much sorrow would have been spared! Around them pressed a hundred noble ladies in beautiful attire; a hundred brave knights in brilliant silks embroidered with threads of gold; and all applauded prowess, encouraging the winners, scorning the cowards and the unsuccessful.

Meanwhile to the list came forward the jousters. There were there some loyal adversaries, some brave champions. Sometimes good lances were bent or broken on mail hauberks, on shields bursting with colors, and of course some of the contestants were thrown into the dust, as some of the good battle horses were forced to flinch.

It happened that one knight was hit and thrown from his saddle so roughly that he remained rigid on the ground, vomiting large bubbles of blood. And when they came to him they found him dead. There followed a great turmoil: some groaned, others consulted; and near relations of the deceased gathered around the body, conducting their loud mourning so that many among the onlookers cried in compassion.

"He was," they said, "a good and joyous knight, and yet so young! He rode here at the wrong hour. Alas! His mother, his fiancée, have fainted. It is pitiful to see them."

Guenolé, hearing this, entered into the field, approached the baron lying on the grass, and he said to those who were there:

"Move aside, in order that I may speak to this man; but first tell me his name."

"His name was Mailoc; he was of a noble family, gallant and loved by all."

The holy abbot knelt on the ground and prayed; and then taking the dead man by the hand, he said to him:

"My brother Mailoc, in the name of Him who created you, I command you to arise."

At these words the knight got up, all full of life, his limbs healthy and whole, smiling as if he had awakened from a sweet dream, and he walked more strongly and able-bodied than ever.

And Guenolé spoke to the people of Ys in these words:

"Believe at last and submit yourselves to God your Lord. Abandon your criminal ways, your pleasures which offend Heaven, and these entertainments through which your souls win only Hell. I say to you, you are like that man as he lay without movement. The word of God will resurrect you as it has resurrected Mailoc, and you will be born to the true life."

Dahut, seeing them hesitant and restrained by the monk, got up, pale and trembling with fury, and she made a sign to two knights who, ready on their chargers, waited at the side of the field. At this sign, they entered at a gallop into the list to make their joust. Guenolé advanced between them; they ran their horses over him and cruelly threw him down.

The recluse got up and, shaking the dust from his robe, he ran to the dais where Gradlon and Dahut, the beautiful, were enthroned. Stretching out his quivering arms, he cried in a terrible voice:

"Wicked king, cowardly and weak king, is it thus you serve God who led you to Corentin in the forest in order to accomplish through you His designs in Cornouaille? I see the crown on your forehead, the sceptre in your hand. These are vain shapes. A woman reigns in your place, and before the crimes of this woman, the saints of paradise veil their faces. Impurity is the name which she bears, idolatry the diamond which shines on her hair, malice the mantle which hides her bosom. Through your weakness God is shamed where He is master. Between Him and you there will be no peace, Gradlon, if you do not this instant chase away from this city your daughter, Dahut, the infamous, the pernicious, and this on behalf of God, king, I order you." Gradlon lowered his eyes and did not reply. However, Dahut fixed on Guenolé her look somber as a storm cloud.

"Monk," she said, "out of my way! That your God gives orders to the rest of the world, I allow. But the city of Ys is mine. No one will speak above me here. No one will be obeyed here except me."

But Guenolé warned her:

"How dare you lift your voice before the messenger of the Lord, woman consecrated to the devil? Return to your mire; return to your bed where sleep with you hideous vices, faults for which there is no longer any pardon: debauchery, incest, sodomy. But cease oppressing these people whom the blood of Christ has redeemed."

And Dahut, laughing and defying him, responded:

"Listen to these people!"

Guenolé lent an ear, and he heard the clamor which mounted to the fences of the field.

"The tournament, the tournament! Let the man of God be thrown out! Let him make room for the brave knights!"

The monk let his head fall to his chest. Tears overran his eyes, running on his rough beard. And, having meditated, he murmured:

"Then be done the will of God! Let the just punishment fall!"

Then from the sky came a powerful voice which said:

"Have you heard how the man of God spoke to Gradlon, in Ys? Do not deliver yourself to love, do not surrender to mad joys; after pleasure comes pain."

"Who eats the flesh of fish will be eaten by fish. Who devours will be devoured, who drinks wine and beer will drink water as a fish; and he who did not know, will know."

The people fled in all directions, and Guenolé left the field and the city.

For a following he had only Mailoc, the knight brought from the dead. He became a monk at Landévenec, and later went to the country of Linhès where he founded a monastery, there leading a dignified and pious life, and dying a holy death.

The Stranger

TOWARD SPRINGTIME A KNIGHT of strange appearance arrived by the high road, with a magnificent retinue. In truth, no prince, no son of emperors had walked toward Ys in such array, nor unfurled such a train of men, horses and wagons. Before him came four heralds, blowing at the crossroads trumpets of ivory; behind came mercenaries, pages, valets and men of arms, all dressed in clothes half black and half the color of fire.

As for the knight, red were his jerkin and his cloak, red his hood, red his horse; his beard and his hair were resplendent as flame; but his color was so pale that blood appeared not to flow in the veins of his cheeks and his forehead; with a singular gleam burned his eyes; his hands were long and fine, pale as his face, and ending in sharp and curling nails.

Those who came across the cortege marveled, and also laughed at the sight of a homely hunchback dwarf wearing a skin of a he-goat, mounted behind the knight.

Gradlon received his guest with great joy, as was his custom, and they found themselves in friendship. Dahut looked thoughtfully at the new arrival and said no word. But suddenly her bold eyes were troubled, and the nearby servants saw her trembling and ready to fall.

The Stranger, when his name was requested of him, pretended gaily that he would not furnish it before a certain date, because of a wager and an oath he had made concerning it.

"My lady," said he to Dahut, "my name is worth nothing if it does not please you. Therefore give me one to your liking; I assure you that it will be dear to me and I shall try to carry it to your honor."

Dahut, the beautiful, smiled at these words.

"Sir knight," she responded, "if I give you a name, despite the fashion in which you came and all this mystery, I would call you 'him whom I await."

"And without a doubt, lady, I would be thus prettily named."

"But no, I shall not do it," said she, "and I shall see if until the end you hold to your wager."

"Ah, beautiful one, should I have to lose it, I would want only that it be here and because of you, as I am conquered by a grace and charm which has no rival."

After this resumed the parties, balls and the feasts. When some time had passed, Dahut questioned the Stranger, taking him aside.

"Sir, are you pleased to be in my city of Ys?"

"My lady," he replied, "how could it not please me, if I contemplate and converse with you here each day? Yet I confess to you that I came here on learning of the entertainments, games, gallantries, and other fine things which are done here at every moment; but I have observed nothing which would not be encountered in cities of less renown and I resent this somewhat, if I may say so."

"I say! Lord knight, did you not admire yesterday that brilliant tournament?"

The Stranger pouted, with disdain.

"To break swords and lances, to run the ring, these are pleasures of children, amusement of pages. Green wreaths, gold ribbons, are these booty for valiant barons?"

"And what booty would better suit them?"

"Your thousand knights, are they not smitten by love?"

"Certainly, they are all in love."

"And with whom? With you, my lady; do they not swear you many oaths?"

"There is not one who, twenty times a day, does not beg me to send him to his death."

"But you treat them as fools, giving them looks, smiles, and hand kisses. Friend, at what a small price you give out your favors. How many among them would pay differently if you so wished."

"What are you saying, sire, and what is your thought?"

"It is that some lovers burn to confront each other for their mistress, not at the arms of a tournament but in the arms of combat. Ah! The stake conquered with so much difficulty by the blade, the sword, the mace, and in the blood of a rival, what is its value for him who receives it or her who gives it!"

At this discourse, Dahut shivered from wicked joy.

"Sire," said she, "you are subtle and of good counsel. This then will my knights do if they love me. From me they will no longer have anything which has not been paid for in blood courageously expended."

From that moment good knights killed each other under the eyes of Dahut and for her pleasure. But still there arrived more from all the countries of the world; for one man murdered, two living ones presented themselves, asking to prove their love by battle and to win some small reward with their life.

Of these challenges, quarrels and slaughters the people of Ys complained and suffered, because it fell to them ceaselessly to pick up the dead, to care for the wounded. This threw them into black humor. And they grumbled that this was a shame and folly to mow down in their youth so many barons and squires.

And the Stranger said to Dahut:

"The wretches reproach you for your amusements. They forget that they hold all they possess from you; that without you, they would be nothing and miserable, living on dried fish, sleeping in caves of the cliffs. Why do you not punish their stupid audacity?"

Then he gave her some advice so that she called together the leading people of the city, hiding her anger and greeting them with courtesy:

"Is it true," she asked, "that through me you are rich and esteemed, provided with beautiful lodging and warm clothes, that your wives and daughters wear gold necklaces, mother-of-pearl bracelets, pendants of coral, that your businesses prosper, and that your coffers are full even in the bad seasons?"

They confessed it, saying:

"Queen, this is your work."

"And for this work," said she with enjoyment, "have I ever asked for payment? Now what would you do for me in exchange?"

"Ah, queen," they responded, seeing her joking manner, "all our goods are yours, at your feet we deposit them."

Gaily Dahut laughed, as in jest.

"I accept them, then," said she. "Tomorrow prepare wagons where each will arrange his gold, his silver, his jewels, his metal vases and his most precious clothing. Harness to these wagons your best horses, place on them your sons and your daughters. I myself shall go out to receive from you this tribute, and to my desires I shall employ it."

Without fear, and lending themselves to this fantasy, the principal people of the city went from door to door.

"Know what you are ordered by Dahut, our beautiful princess."

And they conferred.

"Assuredly she seeks who of us has known how best to profit by her largess, and thinks to give to him in thanks the double of that which he will show. Friends, hide nothing from Dahut."

The next day the people of Ys led onto the port some chariots overflowing with flowers and boughs where they had placed their treasures and assembled the beautiful youth of the city. And at the port they were awaited by certain stable men who quickly excited the horses with blows of the whip and of goads, driving the carriages into the sea, where all was swallowed up.

Later some ambassadors of the king of Vanne came to Ys and said to Gradlon:

"Our master sends greetings and friendship to you. He commands us to bring you this letter."

And here is what was in the letter:

"King Gradlon, a vassal of mine who has grievously injured me has sought refuge in Cornouaille. According to the agreement and the peace that is between us, I request you either to seize him and deliver him to me, or permit my men to enter upon your land and to exact from him prompt justice."

Gradlon assembled his council and said to his faithful:

"Hear this which is asked of me by the king of Vanne, and advise me. What shall I decide upon?"

They responded to him:

"Kings must assist each other. According to the agreement and the peace which is between you, give to the king of Vanne that which he asks of you, because you have many times made similar requests without his ever having refused you."

But the Stranger, learning what was decided in the council, said to Dahut:

"The king of Cornouaille, is he then subject to the king of Vanne?"

"No, lord knight," said Dahut.

"Why then does he allow him passage on his lands? Why return a guest who is trusting in his loyalty? And if the king of Vanne has behaved as a vassal, why should the king of Cornouaille imitate him? In truth, from that the people of Vanne will have a great profit, more than from a victory. They will laugh at you and repeat everywhere that they have made the proud Cornouaillais concede without battle."

Dahut went in haste to the council, where she said the same thing, adding:

"My father, you should declare rebel and disloyal anyone who speaks of handing over his guest."

But an old knight got up and said loudly:

"King, women are of no worth, either in war or in the council. Your faithful think that it is only a traitor who provokes quarrels without gain or glory. Return then, sire, this wicked vassal to the hands of his master and you will give witness not of dependence, but of nobility; and know that doing this you defend your very honor."

Dahut jeered at the old man:

"Sire, white are your hairs. I understand that combats, dangers and fatigues of war tire you. But there are young barons here who have black hair and red blood, and who are not afraid of the men of Vanne."

And compelling Gradlon, she ordered that they write a letter of refusal, to which the ambassadors replied:

"King Gradlon, our master will pass through forcefully; he will hate you and treat you without mercy."

Having taken leave, they returned in shame. The king of Vanne was so angry that he called together a numerous army and waged war cruelly with his neighbors of Cornouaille. Then there was great devastation, killing, rape, sacking of cities and burning of harvest; and there perished without need many good and valiant lords.

The Dance of the Dead

AT GRADLON'S COURT THERE WAS an old knight, virtuous, rich, of pure ideals, and proper spirit. He was called Kebius. It was he who in the council urged that they acknowledge the request of the king of Vanne; but his opinion did not prevail—hence was born that long and evil war.

He had two sons, Hoel and Rivelin, equally wise and esteemed, and they resembled their father so much that people said of them:

"Who is as wise as Kebius? Hoel. Who is as wise as Hoel? Rivelin."

The three were justly indignant at the marks of favor and privilege accorded to the Stranger without name because nothing passed at Ys which that one had not foreseen, disposed, ordained to his fancy. But one day Kebius took aside his sons:

"Children, it is a pity to see an unknown having no title other than a fine face and courage, treated better than a faithful baron. From what country is this man? No one is able to divine, because he knows all parts of the world and speaks all languages. Is he of noble blood? I agree that he has a noble appearance, but his soul is base, his actions are black and false. Since his coming nothing happens except grief, pestilence, misery. The war waged for his pleasure is vain and unhappy. Ah! What weakness is this of King Gradlon. He leaves the sceptre in distaff, he allows a woman to govern us, a stranger to humiliate us. Sons, it seems to me an omen of misfortune for Cornouaille, my heart feels it keenly. All will go badly if we are not careful and find a remedy such as I have envisioned. You have my guarantee that neither hate nor jealousy moves me but only love of our land, and shame to find within the house wicked servants. Are you with me?"

Hoel and Rivelin answered:

"We are with you and agree with that which you have resolved."

"Then," said old Kebius, "we shall deliver the city from this accursed one because there will be no rest at Ys as long as he lives here and is master here. He went today to the country. We shall post ourselves in his way and offer him courteous combat, man against man. We are three; if he kills the first, he will find the second, and if he kills the second, the last will revenge the others; and if we all die there—may God not wish that—at least we will not see the sad things which are in the making here."

The sons agreed. They jumped into the saddle and rode a good distance from the ramparts. The way which the Stranger would follow on his return climbed the cliff, went down into the ravine, intercepted a plain through which passed a large brook. Near this brook, Kebius dismounted and said to Hoel:

"In your role as elder, you will be the first in battle. Urge your horse toward the summit of the cliff. You will watch for the enemy in front of that rock which overhangs the road. Go and guard yourself, because he is strong and clever."

Hoel galloped toward the crest. And the old man called Rivelin.

"You will hide yourself in the ditch at the bottom of the ravine. If the Stranger forces his passage against Hoel, he will descend the slope at a gallop; place yourself in his way and stop him. Son, you are less strong than your brother but more supple and artful. Wait for the favorable moment. Save your breath, do not press too near the enemy, but when he lifts up his arm slip your sword into him under the armpit while turning aside your horse."

He embraced his son, whom he cherished more tenderly than the other. Alas! Would that he suspected who his rival was! Rivelin left and lay hidden at the designated place under some walnut trees. As for the old knight, he tied his mount to a nearby tree and positioned himself by the ford of the brook, and he thought:

"Hoel is robust, Rivelin is skillful, but youth is hot tempered and foolhardy, swift to fatal mistakes. Kebius has two sons, beautiful and noble, and he is looked at with envy; this evening, perhaps he will be pitied as an ill-fated father."

He fell into dark thoughts. His beard spread out on his chest like brilliant snow. He thought again:

"The father will not survive his sons. If the wicked one defeats the younger men, how will he ever succumb before the old? And yet my arm was of steel, my body of bronze, on me swords were blunted, maces broken; my enemies feared me, my friends respected me as the most brave and the most fortunate in battle. Alas! That time is far gone! Shamed be the age which has bent my height and stiffened my limbs. But why sadden myself? My sons are strong fighters, and if they weaken, I shall find again my former strength to conquer."

Only toward evening did the Stranger return following the line of the cliff. When he was on the crest he perceived a knight barring his way. It was Hoel who sprang up on him:

"Sire, it is necessary to cross swords. One of us will remain on the plain. Therefore defend yourself, I beg you, because I shall not spare you."

And he charged him, his weapon raised high. The Stranger stopped his horse, and suddenly between Hoel and him a deep trench opened up, as if a thunderbolt had touched the soil, as if the mountain had split. The Cornouaille charger lost its footing. Hoel was thrown against a rock which split open his skull, scattering his brains about. He fell lifeless in the dust.

The Stranger had not even drawn his sword, nor made a movement. When he saw Hoel stretched in the dust, he gave spur to his horse and rode off quickly. But in the ravine was Rivelin who from afar cried to him:

"Hoel is dead. Ah, felon! By my hand you will perish."

And he darted forth, the valiant son. Then from the ground under him shot up a flame so powerful that it enveloped both horse and man, lifting itself to the tops of the walnut trees which bordered the route. And the horse, in fury, bounded to the right and to the left carrying Rivelin, both burning as torches of resin, as stacks of straw.

More quickly toward the plain galloped the Stranger. Old Kebius, seated on a stone at the ford of the brook, saw him emerge from the sunken road. When he recognized the red charger and the red cloak, a great pain grasped him. He cried and tore at his breast:

"Alas! Through arrogance I have lost my children. I must have the strength to punish the murderer. After that, willingly will I die."

And he said to the Stranger who was approaching the ford:

"Dismount. It is necessary to complete your task. I shall fight with honor and loyalty as have my sons."

The Stranger crossed his arms and smiled. Ah, his smile was such that the old man paled with anger and, beside himself, he struck his sword at the chest of the horse; and the blow was so powerful that it would have pierced a wall. But a wonder occurred. The sword broke cleanly through the middle, as a frail stick. Kebius took up his lance and aimed; the lance broke at the handle. He groaned and sought to strike with his hand, but his arm fell inert. The old knight was seized with despair:

"Cursed be the sorcerer! His horse is enchanted, his body is covered with invisible armor. Ah, this is certainly the reason my good sons are dead!"

And the unhappy man plunged his knife into his flesh; he fell at the side of the brook whose ripples were tainted with blood; his white hairs clung to the clumps of reeds.

Meanwhile, in her castle, Dahut languished and sighed. Ah! How her haughty face was bowed, how her eyes were veiled with care. She no longer laughed her beautiful laugh; she groaned and sought darkness. From these signs she understood that she was in love. And whom did she love? The Stranger, he who entered into Ys without a name, of whom no one knew either his home or his birth.

Strolling under the trees, in the garden filled with the night, she meditated:

"All those who have seen me, desire me. All those to whom I have spoken have consecrated to me their souls; but my heart, tumultuous as the sea, was as cold as the sea. Weariness was the companion of my caprice. The gentle knights who have held me in their arms were suffocated by the mask, the man in black has thrown them across his horse, Plogoff has swallowed them. Nonetheless, having known the kisses of Dahut for an entire night, their fate is enviable. But how many others, scorned or wearied of my demands, drag on their odious life and die of their pain? Ah, now love takes revenge and tortures me.

"This Stranger, what secret power has he which binds and subjugates me? At his voice, my heart stops beating, my bones melt, all my being is overwhelmed. He orders, I obey; he looks at me, I belong entirely to him. Dahut, proud Dahut, to what master have you given yourself? He is indifferent to your love, he is unaware of it, and still all reveals it at each hour, your words and your silences, your impulses, that which you scorn; because in vain you have tried to close up in yourself this consuming ardor. No one is insensitive to it; he alone is blind and deaf. Or perhaps he wishes to neither see nor hear. What shall I do? Shall I attempt to seduce him, to entreat him to have mercy? I have a thousand snares to conquer lovers. How could he resist? But what if he does resist, if he spurns me and scoffs at me! Ah, poor Dahut!"

Thus lamented the beautiful princess, wandering under the branches in the falling evening.

Suddenly the Stranger was before her. In the semidarkness his cloak and his beard seemed to flame; his eyes gleamed as stars on a moonless night. Dahut gazed upon him, admiring, and she shivered from agony and from love, while he greeted her courteously.

"My lady, in this pretty garden, what dreams do you have thus alone?"

She turned away her head, not responding. They walked side by side under the low boughs where the birds slept, and Dahut emboldened herself to say:

"Sire, shall I tell you that which makes me thoughtful? Something about you assuredly astonishes me."

"Is that true, friend? If it is an omission, I shall make up for it; if it is some mistake, I shall remedy it."

"Friend," said Dahut, "is it not through your counsel that the knights of my court joust at great risks, with the lance, the mace and the sword, so much that many of them have perished or suffer grave wounds?"

"From me was the counsel and by the agreement of your knights; because the conquerors have sweet rewards, receiving them from you, and no one has found the battle too hard."

"No one, unless it be you, sire."

"What are you saying, Dahut, my beautiful friend?"

"That in this battle you do not take part. How many times I have watched for you, thinking to recognize you, a baron, skillful and valiant. Never have your features appeared before me under the raised helmet of the conqueror."

"Ah! Do not accuse me of cowardice!"

"Sire, how could I? Your arrow reaches the bird in the clouds, your sword deals death to the wild boar; none has more cleverness and courage than you. Yet you do not solicit what you call these high rewards which one has from me, you leave them to others without regret."

To these words, the Stranger answered:

"It is better not to seek them, my lady, than to see them given to anyone who comes along."

Ah! How the heart of Dahut palpitated and suffered. This response, is it a jest? Is it a hidden avowal? She touched the hand of the knight, that hand burned with excitement, without a doubt.

"Sire, your hand burns as the fire."

"Friend, all burns in me and around me. Have a care."

Joyously Dahut squeezed herself against him.

"Ah! I wish to be consumed by that fire, if it is not a lie. But what do I know of you, in whom there is only mystery. Extremely clever, he who would know you from your words, very unwise, he who would judge you by your actions. You resemble other men as little as the sun resembles the candle. You possess the seven arts of magic, you read stars and faces, you change the base metals into gold, gross wool into silk, you have drugs which subdue horses, and you have eyes which subjugate the wildest souls."

"Beautiful one, that is little," said the Stranger, laughing. "I am equal to more, and I shall prove it to you, for if it please you, I shall make the dead dance before you. A little while ago, on my way, I found in ambush old Kebius and his two sons. They attacked me to their undoing. All three

were immediately slain, well punished and giving up their last breath."

"Sire," said Dahut, "that is good news; they detested me vilely, showing their disapproval and offering criticism in all things."

"But friend, against their will they shall amuse themselves this evening, they will frolic and dance with us; is that not on our part a friendly game, a courteous revenge?"

In the evening into the great salon came ladies, maidens, knights, and pages, those who at Dahut's command sported and frolicked with her, often until dawn. And they noticed this night that there was in the hall neither music nor musicians, only a hunchback dwarf blowing into his bagpipes. It was the dwarf whom the Stranger had carried on the back of his horse when he first entered Ys. The foolish people surrounded him and heckled him.

"Hail, beautiful fiddler, are you conducting the devil's nuptials? What step will you teach us? Is this the dance of the Korrigans under the moon?"

At the first stroke of midnight the dwarf began to play a dance. Everyone fell silent. They listened to a tune which was fast and jerky, which no one had ever heard. Suddenly at these strange sounds, a terrible anguish seized them, a shiver went through their bones and chilled their blood. They gazed at each other and they saw themselves, pale and drawn, trembling on their legs. And then, unattended, the doors opened. Three dancers appeared, fastened together by a chain, their arms entwined, hand in hand. It was Kebius, it was Hoel, it was Rivelin.

The old baron was barechested, a knife buried there up to the handle; the blood spurted out, soiling the silk tunic, sticking to the hairs of the long white beard. Hoel the brave showed his skull split, his face crushed, his clothes stained with mud and full of large holes. Rivelin the gentle son is all stripped, the body black and dried by fire, the skin torn to shreds. The unlucky ones! They advanced, turning and drawing back to the rhythm of the dance, their eyes extinguished, their nerves shriveled by death, and their feet striking the stone floor with a horrible sound of clinking bones.

At this spectacle, a silence of dread weighed on the bystanders. They wished to flee yet were unable to move. They wished to cry out and their mouths uttered no sound.

Only Dahut laughed and joked, seated under the canopy, the Stranger beside her.

"Ah, sire, what a joyous dance! These good dead have elegant form! How elegant and gracious is their dance!"

"Friend," he answered, "what will you say when you see this whole group dancing behind them?"

He gave the hunchback dwarf a sign and the dwarf started to play in such a manner that, through marvel and witchcraft, ladies and knights paired up against their will, and all the assembly began to dance, following Kebius, Hoel and Rivelin, and this was a marvel to wonder at, the grinning faces of these handsome knights, of these merry maidens. Ah! No one of them took pleasure in it. The horror painted itself on their faces, in their haggard eyes; and little by little their bodies became cold and rigid as those of the three dead; they walked and turned as if statues of stone.

The hours passed and the dwarf continued to blow into his bagpipes, and the music became brisker and more jerky. Already the dancers were tired, the sweat ran in large drops down their foreheads; some uttered sharp cries, others moaned quietly. Soon the round picked up speed; it was as if a furious whirlwind traversed the hall, shaking the walls, with the sound of a storm in the trees.

Near was the dawn. Suddenly from afar the cock crowed. At this signal, by itself for the second time the door opened, and springing forth into the lightening night, the infernal dancers disappeared from view, following the hunchback musician behind the three dead.

None of those who danced that dance ever returned.

The Keys of Silver

DAHUT, THE BEAUTIFUL PRINCESS, was tormented by her desire. Her hair was dishevelled, her cheeks inflamed by fever, her eyelids swollen from lack of sleep. She chased away her squires, her pages, her master cook, who wished to amuse her. She beat the servants who consoled her. Under an outstretched canopy she cried, lamenting her desperation.

"Love is tearing me apart, love is killing me; I cannot stand it any longer. If he whom I love is not mine I shall die. Ah, how he scorns me and laughs at my sorrow! Have I not made my avowal to him? Have I not held his hand in mine? Has he not guessed my thoughts through my looks? And what thoughts, were they buried at the depth of my heart, could be hidden from him? May he love me at last, may he caress me in his arms, may he take me entirely, may he deliver me from my illness! Then I shall revenge myself as well. But now I do not know what to do, for he has seduced and bewitched me."

And she sought in her mind how to attract the pitiless one. She created a hundred projects that she abandoned in turn.

"But I must do something," she thought. "I shall send him the magic mask, which obliges him to love me and to give himself to me."

She decided and called the man in black, her secret messenger of love; but the man was not at the chateau and nobody knew of him.

"Oh, well!" said Dahut to herself. "I shall do it alone."

At once she wrote some tender words, full of sweet reproaches:

"Lover who holds my heart, will you not cease to treat it without pity or care? Alas! I am pierced by it, and my plight will draw tears from you. If you do not wish me to perish, this evening present yourself at the small door of the cliff. And I beg you, please, take this mask of silk so that no one will suspect you. If you do not come, friend, tomorrow you will see me dead."

She confided these words and the magic mask to a trustworthy girl and ordered her to deliver them. Then she dressed and perfumed her hair; she put on slippers of leather, she adorned herself in a tunic of fine cloth embroidered with gold; she chose her richest jewels. How beautiful she appeared in this finery!

The day passed. At dusk, Dahut impatiently ran to the place of rendez-vous; the Stranger was there, but without the mask!

"Ah, sire, what have you done? Assuredly on your way someone will have recognized you—to my shame."

The Stranger answered:

"What is the need of a mask, when already each of us wears one?

At these words, she gazed at him frightened.

"It pleases you frequently to speak thus to me words I do not under-stand. But from you I allow everything. Follow me, because to linger here is perilous—there is great danger of being discovered."

She led him toward her chamber, ornamented with deep bed covers of wool and of fur, of thick rugs, cushions of scarlet. Columns of jasper and marble supported the ceiling, a spring of water sang in a silver basin.

Then Dahut sat down at the feet of the Stranger.

"Many would want," said he, "to contemplate thus Dahut the proud, who only endured lovers at her knees."

"I no longer remember that," said she. "Before now I have not lived."

The Stranger smiled into his beard of flame.

"Ah, my lady, what a marvelous love is that!"

"Friend, you ridicule me still. Nevertheless I shall tell you why I cherish you thus, and perhaps then you will believe me. I was a child when the king my father took me to the tomb of the holy recluse Guethenoc, where miracles occurred; I perceived at the entrance a lord of handsome stature. He had as you do a red cloak, and a red hood, his beard and his hair were the color of yours, and he had your teasing and gentle air, also a face, strange and noble as yours, which no one forgets. And I asked King Gradlon: 'Father, who is that knight standing there?' Astonished, my father looked at me: 'Daughter, what do you say? There is there only white stone, only green cypress.' But I saw him and toward him I advanced. When I extended my arm to touch him, he disappeared. I felt under my fingers only the cold white stone of the sepulcher. Later, sire, I questioned on this subject an old bard who lived near the palace playing the harp to amuse the king and singing some lays. This old man knew the beginning and the end of all things; he went into the moors where stand the sacred stones, and upon returning he said to me, 'Dahut, guard yourself from him whom you saw at the tomb of Guethenoc. If he

approaches you, flee! If he follows you, hide yourself and do not let him discover you because from him will come to you tears, ruin and death.' Then imagine, at your arrival, what was my confusion! I immediately recalled the old bard, and the idea of flight took possession of me. But as soon as you had spoken, my heart, through enchantment, was calmed. I smiled at you. When you asked me to give you a name, do you recall my response? 'You are he whom I have awaited.' From that moment, lord, I was yours."

"Then," said the Stranger, "despite the advice of the bard you had no fear?"

Dahut did not know fear no matter what the outcome. Passionately she brushed the Stranger with her fine hair. And he, into this beautiful crown of hair, slipped his pale hand with the pointed nails. Suddenly a muffled sound came up from the sea and a terrible gust of wind hurled itself against the walls, breaking through the windows, tearing away the heavy curtain, knocking over the copper candlesticks. Dahut, alarmed, implored her friend:

"Sire, I beg you, mount the tower and look at the Ocean."

The Stranger obeyed and he returned saying: "The sky is grey as lead, the Ocean seethes, the wind of death whistles in the rocks, the frightened sea-birds whirl about on the shore."

"Oh!" cried Dahut. "That is the sign of a storm. Friend, this evening the Ocean is going to become furious through resentment and jealousy. You should know that before knowing you, I loved only the sea; I gave him my soul and my flesh, I caressed him and kissed him each day; he submitted to me as does the most tender servant. All my lovers except the sea occupied me only for the joy of the hour, for a swift embrace, for a night without a morrow, and the Ocean, my only true love, was not jealous of them because to him I delivered their inert bodies in the abyss of Plogoff. All of them I abandoned to the sea without regret; the valiant ones full of glory and honor who showed me their wounds received for my sake, the young knights, thirsty for adventures, who sought in my eyes the star of their fortune, the timid, blushing squires who cried under my kisses. Friend, all of them I have thrown to the Ocean, and he erased from them, as he saw fit, the trace of my lips. But you! He understands that my love has left him, and he growls, he threatens. It doesn't matter; to you, not to him, I now belong."

Outside, the storm worsened, beating the castle as a ram of war. On its granite foundation, the high rock trembled.

"Friend," said Dahut, "climb again to the tower and see what the Ocean does."

He climbed to the tower, soon redescending.

"The wind wished to throw me down; all is black and sinister; the sound of the Ocean is that of a thousand chariots on the pavement, a thousand trees hurled down from the mountain. The columns of waves scale the cliff, lifting themselves to the clouds."

Dahut smiled with pride.

"Let him bellow and assail us! The dikes built by the Korrigans face him; the gates of bronze are well closed, and only King Gradlon has the silver keys which open the sea."

"Oh!" said the Stranger. "Gradlon has only Cornouaille for his king-dom, yet he is more powerful than the Roman emperor since he commands the Ocean."

And toward Dahut he bent:

"Beauty, who loves me so much, for my pleasure what will you do?"

"To please you, my lord, I will do violence or prowess, I will be fool or wise, I would kill your rival or kiss him at your will."

"Then, friend, if I ask it of you would you give me the silver keys which open the sea?"

Dahut shuddered. An extreme pallor covered her face.

"Ah, sire, that which you ask, I am not able to accord you. The keys are King Gradlon's and hang at his neck; day and night, he never leaves them!"

"On his bed, the king sleeps peacefully. To take from his neck the keys of silver would be easy prowess, Dahut!"

She bowed, as a flower bent by the storm, and did not answer. Then arising to satisfy her friend, her legs gave way, and she fell onto the pillows.

"Ah, I am not able to bring myself to do it." she murmured. "You see this weakness; in truth, this is a sad omen."

Then the Stranger raised her up and spoke thus into her ear:

"If you do my will, I will tell you my name, the name kept hidden from all, which no one for his own good must know. It is beautiful and terrible as the night, it resounds as the trumpet, it dazzles as a flash of lightning. Dahut, when you know who embraces you, your heart will burst from joy and from pride. And when you have surrendered to me the keys which open the sea we shall depart, you and I; into my kingdom I shall lead you. Because I have an immense kingdom; it surpasses the limits of the earth, it is more vast than the sky, its subjects are more numerous than the fish of the sea, than the birds of the forest. One sees there hills of gems, palaces of diamonds, rivers rolling with sands of gold. There I inhabit a palace of fire, with columns of smoke; under a canopy of rubies rises my throne of crystal. Friend, in this country, you will be queen and mistress, if you take the silver keys and give them to me according to my desire."

But Dahut said:

"Keep your name, sire, and your treasures. I wish only to be loved; and perhaps you will love me when I have betrayed my father and my faith, when I have placed in your hands the fate of my city. Come then, let us make haste."

She led him from room to room into the chamber of Gradlon. Now whoever might have looked upon the old king on his bed would have been filled with admiration, he was so handsome and dignified in his scarlet cloak with his white hair covering his shoulders, and his beard of snow, with the chain of gold around his neck. And anyone hiding in the shadow would have seen the young daughter making her way toward the old king on bare feet with muffled steps; at the head of her sleeping father she stopped, her courage failed her, the horror of her crime made her hesitate. But the Stranger entered the room after her, and he encouraged her. He commanded in a low voice:

"Dahut, Dahut, the keys."

She bent over, she knelt down: with nimble fingers without waking the king she took off the chain of gold on which hung the keys of silver, the keys which open the sea.

Immediately the roaring of the storm became stronger, the fall of the water on the rocks resounded in the courts and the large halls. And now Dahut, the fearless, started at each sound. Fright overtook her, she fled along the dark corridors.

"Friend," said she, reeling, "here are the keys. Alas! A mortal cold flows in my veins, an inconquerable fear oppresses me."

"Dahut, that is the crash of the Ocean which vexes you; at daybreak your fright will pass away."

"Ah! Sire, now I am in anguish. Climb once again to the tower, and tell me if this storm is not about to end, if dawn has not begun to appear."

The Stranger, in haste, climbed the stairs of the tower. Dahut followed him, but at a distance because she could scarcely breathe and her limbs gave way. Ah! The darkness weighed on her. How she longed for the coming of light!

At last she arrived at the summit. From the heavens overcast with clouds no light descended. Dahut called her friend. She extended her arms to reach him, to touch him in the darkness; she felt only the coldness of the air, only the dripping of the rain.

"Sire, where are you? Why have you left me thus?"

An immense flash of lightning rent the sky. Dahut looked all around her: nobody! But on the paving stone where she moved forward she saw a black spot deeply marked in the stone, the form of which was that of the foot of a he-goat.

The Punishment

"THE GATES ARE OPEN! . . . the water is rising! . . . the water is rising!"

In the night this clamor flew across the city. But he who uttered it did not repeat it. He who heard it did not hear it a second time, so rapid was the invasion of the sea.

Within his castle slept King Gradlon in his cloak of scarlet, his white beard hiding his chest, his white hair flowing over his shoulders. The waves shaking the ramparts awoke him. He opened his eyes. At some distance from his bed a vivid light shone, a bright halo in the middle of which was a man clothed in the skin of a wild ox and with a belt of branches; the face of this man was somber and sad, his fist grasped a knotty staff. And Gradlon recognized Guenolé, the abbot of Landévenec, the holy recluse.

And Guenolé, advancing toward the king, spoke thus:

"Get up, lord, get up! The sea overflows, the dike is broken! Make haste to flee on horseback!"

Gradlon, without moving, responded:

"Good monk, what are you doing here in this place at this hour?"

Guenolé said: "God, through His goodness and miracle has sent me to you because Ys, your city, is condemned, all who live here are to perish. But you, you have sinned through weakness and love, not through malice, and you will be saved. Nevertheless, do not tarry. Already the water encroaches upon the courtyards, the water is washing your door."

The king shook his head, smiling.

"Ah, you are but a phantom of my dreams, I understand it well because of this speech. The dike is impregnable; in my presence the bronze doors were closed this evening; I have closed my city to the sea, how may the sea enter it? Holy one, leave Gradlon to his repose!"

"Oh, king, the doors you closed this evening are now open to the Ocean. At your neck you had suspended the silver keys held by a chain of gold, and the keys and the chain are no longer in their place."

To his neck the king reached his hand.

"Oh monk, you speak the truth; the keys have been stolen during my sleep. I am lost!"

Guenolé repeated softly:

"God has received you in His mercy, Gradlon, for all the chapels and all the monasteries you built at Quimper, and for Landévenec where so many of His humble servants are living, praying and mortifying themselves. So then do not hesitate; soon it will be too late."

Gradlon sprang from his bed. He ran from the palace even as the sea was tearing out the steps. He reached the stable where Morvark, the black horse with the flaming nostrils, pawed the ground and neighed with anger. The king jumped on the back of the stallion, who carried him out of the castle.

Morvark, the valiant charger, swam without fatigue close to the beach; across the inundated squares, the streets like torrents, he galloped lighter than air; and Gradlon felt his heart half-relieved, then, looking back, he saw that the Ocean followed him closely as the hunter follows the doe or the hare; he struck the horse with his heel and thinking of his beloved daughter, he groaned:

"Dahut, where are you at this moment? What has happened to you?"

Morvark, urged on by the waves which made under his feet a thick carpet of foam, went back and forth within the ramparts, going over the same path a hundred times. Again and again he passed the castle whose terraces and lodgings the tide covered, of which only the roof of lead and high walls still emerged. Then from the darkness came a lamentable voice:

"Father! Father! Save me!"

It was the voice of Dahut. She was at the summit of a tower, Dahut whom the enormous waves threatened and whose white robe floated in the wind; in her hair the water flowed, her trembling hands made a gesture of appeal.

"Daughter, here I am."

Gradlon directed the good horse toward the tower. He extended his arms. Dahut reached him, jumping on behind, her body soaking and shivering, from her mouth escaped a sad lamentation.

"Father, have mercy on me."

But scarcely was she on the horse than he flinched as if three heavily armed men had mounted him. The Ocean reached him, clasped him, with a blow that shook him to his shins; Gradlon felt his knees grow cold; his fingers clasped the hair of Morvark. The noble animal beat the seas with his

powerful hoofs; boldly his breast split the swells as the prow of a ship under the regular effort of the oars; he neighed from pride and from rage and, lifting up his double burden, he shook his wet mane. Nevertheless the water licked his sweating flank, penetrated his flaming nostrils. The riders were engulfed up to their waists.

The king shivered and cried. His daughter, clinging to his shoulders, without ceasing begged him:

"Father, father, the Ocean wants to seize me! Save me from him!"

All at once the point of a rock brightened; a vivid light shot forth, similar to that which Gradlon perceived in the night in his chamber. There again in the middle of it was the abbot of Landévenec.

"Gradlon, Gradlon, you are destroying yourself! If you wish to live, reject the demon who is behind you."

The king opened his eyelids, burning with salt; he waved his dripping arms over his head.

"Holy man, what do you say? What do you ask? Behind me there is only my daughter. I love her more than life; with her I shall die if it is necessary."

The horse swam near the rock. Gradlon saw the monk leaning toward the sea, his staff clasped in his right hand, his clothes of animal skin torn by the storm. Around him, in marvelous array, shone the halo of light; under black eyebrows flared his eyes; his voice made the waves silent:

"Gradlon, Gradlon, if you fear God, keep no longer mounted behind you your daughter whom you cherish so much. It is through her that Ys your city is ruined and given to the Ocean; she has surrendered her body to everyone, her soul to the Enemy of God, and God is wearied of her, and has judged her. The silver keys that hung around your neck, she stole them, lord king, while you slept. The doors have been opened. The sea has entered and the hand of God has been lifted to punish. Listen to me. Reject the impure one, the accursed one; she is promised to the Ocean. There is time yet for you, Gradlon, to be pardoned."

The old king felt a cruel pain, his soul grieved, he sobbed and could not speak. The water continued to rise; it reached his chest; his white beard floated among the foam, and while Guenolé solemnly called upon him, he felt Dahut so tightly clinging that he could not shake her off if he wished to. In truth, he did not wish it, he could not. She was his beloved daughter, flesh of his flesh, she who on the waves was born of Malgven, his beautiful queen.

Then when Morvark was near to sinking into the abyss, Guenolé extended his right arm. With his staff he touched Dahut on her shoulder, which was bare since the cords of her robe had come untied. He touched Dahut with his staff, and she fell over. Separating her hands, she let go of Gradlon, and slipped into the sea, which seized her and closed over her.

At the same instant, as if delivered from all burden, Morvark returned to the surface, taking again his rapid course. And as the waves subsided before him, he galloped as easily as on a path of soft earth, as on the tender grass of a pasture. Not far from there was a high headland. Morvark attained it, and Gradlon, having dismounted, fell to his knees to praise God.

When he had prayed, he turned his thoughts to Dahut, his beloved daughter, whose eyes and smile the savage Ocean had extinguished, and whose beautiful body was now torn apart on the reefs. And the old king, crying bitterly, held himself up against the cliff to look at the place where formerly was seen the opulent and noisy city of Ys. He saw only the sky, suddenly calm and free of clouds, and below, a bay as tranquil as a lake in which is reflected the pale fire of the stars.